GOD'S
AMAZING JOURNEY
and
FAITHFULNESS

GOD'S
AMAZING JOURNEY
and
FAITHFULNESS

RON BYSTROM *with* CHAR BYSTROM

XULON PRESS

Xulon Press
2301 Lucien Way #415
Maitland, FL 32751
407.339.4217
www.xulonpress.com

Unless otherwise indicated, Scripture quotations taken from the New American Standard Bible (NASB). Copyright © 1960, 1962, 1963, 1968, 1971, 1972, 1973, 1975, 1977, 1995 by The Lockman Foundation. Used by permission. All rights reserved.

Printed in the United States of America.

ISBN-13: 978-1-6305-0138-9

TABLE OF CONTENTS

PREFACE

———————◇———————

I ntrigued.
   Shocked.
   Anxious.
   Laughing.
   Saying **"No Way!"**

We hope these words describe a few of the emotions and responses you experience as you read about the **amazing journey** God had planned for your Grandmom and me.

Psalm 145:4 says, "One generation shall praise Your works to another, and shall declare Your mighty acts."

That is what this book is all about. (For those of you who would not call us Grandmom and Granddad, you will quickly notice that this book was written specifically to our grandkids. But it can also relate to you).

The pages of what you are about to read are filled with stories of God's mighty acts and His faithfulness to us as we simply walked with Him. We hope and pray that it will help you in your journey towards fulfilling every purpose God has for you including:

- not just knowing in your head what is true about God, but knowing Him personally and intimately
- experiencing His love daily

- loving and worshipping Him with all your heart, soul, mind, and strength
- living the life of adventure which God intends for you while fulfilling the good works He has prepared for you,
- realizing that knowing Him, living for Him and His glory, is the greatest gift we can ever receive in this life
-increasingly growing in your trust in His amazing power, love, grace, and Truths.

We would like to make a **special request** of you as our grand-kids. We would like to ask you to read this book at least four times: When you are around ten, seventeen, twenty-one, and thirty years of age. Why? As you reach these ages you will be experiencing new and different freedoms, choices, and challenges in life. The meaning, insights, and application points you may gain from our life stories will most likely be quite different for you at those times in your life.

As you face the unknown, insecurities, or difficult circum-stances, God will want to reveal more of who He is and who He wants to be in and through your life. We pray that the challenges we faced and how God demonstrated His faithfulness to us will give you hope, encouragement, endurance, and wisdom.

I (Granddad) also wanted to share something very personal as you begin to read this book. It relates to how I viewed myself as a teenager and a college student. If there was one word that would describe how I viewed myself, that word would be mediocre. As I looked at who I was in every area of my life that seemed to be where I fell. Academically, I did not excel but did okay as an A-/ B+ student: mediocre. In sports, I was coordinated and better than a lot of kids, but I wasn't good enough to make the varsity team in any sport in high school: mediocre. Socially I had an okay group of friends and we enjoyed going to dances, going to the Jersey shore and meeting girls, but I was far from being a part of the cool group of kids in school: mediocre. As I went to college, the theme of being mediocre continued and was reinforced in almost every area of my life.

However, as you read this book, I believe you will join me in concluding that my/our lives have ended up being **anything but mediocre.** If you view yourself in any way as I saw myself, mediocre, please do not underestimate what God can do through you if you only walk humbly and intimately with Him.

We are amazed, humbled, surprised, and at times, we have to laugh as we consider the life we have experienced since we began to know and follow our amazing Heavenly Father.

We pray that you will enjoy, laugh, and be astounded as you see our imaginative God at work.

Love,
Granddad and Grandmom

Acknowledgement

———◇———

C har and I would like to express our sincere thanks to our good friend Bob Smiley, a Princeton University graduate who was active as a student within the Cru movement. Bob is the author of two books, a writer and a producer for both TV shows and films. We are forever grateful to Bob for his encouraging words, his wise counsel, and his gracious effort in editing this book.

Chapter 1

FILLED WITH FEAR!

———— ⋊ ————

I t was May 1986. Months of seeking the Lord and prayer had occurred. Your Grandmom and I were about to lead a team into the communist country of Romania. Under communism, millions of people lived in a state of fear. If words were spoken in opposition to the government, or if Christians became too verbal about their faith in Christ, they could spend years in prison or have their children removed from their homes and placed in state-run orphanages. Though these realities existed with varying degrees in Russia and other communist countries, it was especially true in Romania. Most people lived in a state of oppression, depression, and fear. Yet, this was the country to which CCC (formerly **C**ampus **C**rusade for **C**hrist – now **C**ru.) leadership had challenged us to go.

What we experienced as we followed our Lord behind the Iron Curtain dramatically changed our lives.

Grandmom, Michelle (eleven), Jen (nine), Kristi (six), and I flew into Vienna, Austria, for a briefing conference with the 37 students and staff members we were leading into Romania. At the briefing, where teams gathered just prior to departure, we were informed that if any of our teams stayed in a location more than seven to ten days, it was virtually guaranteed that they would be taken in by the police or Securitate (the KGB of Russia/FBI of the

USA) and be interrogated. As a result, special training was given on how to answer questions and respond to the intimidating accusations that might be screamed at us.

We also learned that everyone except our family would be entering Romania by train. Those entering Romania by train were told to expect every piece of clothing and every item in their backpacks to be taken out and inspected. As a Bible would be found, we were given instructions on how to answer questions related to why this was in our possession. As a family, we (Grandmom, me, Michelle, Jennifer, and Kristi) would drive into Romania in a gray Volvo. Having a car would provide greater freedom for us as a family, which seemed good. But we were also told that when we attempted to cross the border from Hungary into Romania, **we could expect at least a two-to-three-hour delay. Border guards would probably search every piece of clothing in our suitcases. They might also take everything out of the trunk and inspect it**.

After this orientation, the Cru leadership asked to speak to your Grandmom and me to make a request. As we met, they asked us to smuggle a copy of the *JESUS* film translated into Romanian, a large movie projector (15" high, 9" wide, and 13" long), and a number of Christian articles that had been translated into Romanian into the country. One more detail shared was that the *JESUS* film was copied onto three large projector reels, each placed in an 18"x18"x 2" encasement. Obviously, along with the movie projector, this was something that could be easily noticed during a border inspection. It wasn't exactly something one could easily hide!

Having digested what they just told us to expect at the border crossing, in shock I responded, "Are you kidding me?"

They were not kidding!

They simply said, **"This is what we do. We trust the Lord to get things through."**

Troubled and amazed that our leadership would ask us to do this, I shared, "I am sorry. We can't just say yes to this. It isn't just me smuggling something into Romania. I have Char and our three daughters. What will happen if the border guards find these things?"

They explained, "There are three possibilities. They could interrogate you, confiscate everything, and let you enter the country. They could interrogate you, confiscate everything, and refuse your entry into the country. Or, they could interrogate you, and we really do not know what might happen."

Surprised, perplexed, and still somewhat shocked, we told them we would have to seek the Lord before we could say "Yes."

As you might imagine, your Grandmom and I spent a good part of that night praying about what we should do. In the morning, we took time to discuss what we were thinking. As we struggled with the decision, we both came to four conclusions.

First, we were confident that God had led us to lead this mission.

Second, the body of Christ in Romania had a significant need for these items.

Third, we were going under the authority that God had placed over us.

And fourth, those leaders had asked us to trust God with this situation.

While meeting with the Cru leadership later that morning, we said, "Okay, we will trust God and do this."

The day before we left Vienna for Romania, we searched the local markets and bought a seven-week supply of fruit juices, cereal, and powdered milk to supplement our food while in-country. These items were added to the vitamins, minerals, and other nutritional foods that we brought from the US because of the report that the fruits and vegetables in Romania would be contaminated by the radioactive fallout from the meltdown of the nuclear reactor in the Ukraine (more about this later).

As we packed the car, we put the movie projector, the *JESUS* film cases, and the translated articles in the trunk. Then we put all the food items on top of them. Our five suitcases, one for each of us, were secured on the roof rack. Before we departed, as we got into the car, we prayed, "God, please guide us and lead us on this trip. May You be glorified through everything we do. Give us a fun summer together. May Your hand protect us. In Jesus' name, Amen."

The drive to the Austrian-Hungarian border was only a couple hours. True to what we had been told, we went through the border into communist Hungary without an extended search of the car or many questions. For this we were thankful and relieved. We drove the rest of the day through northern Hungary, stayed in a hotel that night, and planned to enter Romania the next morning.

As we drove away from the hotel the following morning, I was filled with apprehension. Visions of guards surrounding us, being harshly interrogated, and worst-case scenarios of what could happen to us/to our girls played over and over in my mind. Miles before we arrived at the Romanian border, traffic was backed up. Again, what we had been told was true. Border guards were searching through the cars and trucks, and that meant it would take hours to cross the border. The longer we waited the more uneasy and scared I became. I didn't want the girls to be concerned, so I tried to suppress my emotions, act normal, and stay involved in talking or listening as Grandmom read a book.

Finally we reached the dreaded border guards. As different lines of cars formed, I attempted to guess who would search the car in which line. We had been told that the women border guards tended to be more thorough in their search, so if at all possible, we should get in a line with a male guard. Slowly I crept over to where it appeared that a male border guard was stationed. We stopped. I got out of the car. Grandmom and the girls stayed in the car. A large guard, probably about 6 foot-2 inches, weighing about 235 lbs. (unusually tall and big for a Romanian), with dark hair walked up. He pointed to the suitcases on top of the car and asked for our passports. As I took the suitcases off the roof, he disappeared with our passports. After a few minutes he returned and began opening each of the suitcases. Every piece of clothing was picked up to see if something was hidden in between the items. I expected that he would do this for your Grandmom's and my suitcase. But then he began to do the same for the suitcases of all three girls. The longer he looked, as the thoroughness of his search continued, fear grew within me. I was praying like crazy. "Oh God. Don't let him go through the trunk like this."

I tried to act calm and normal, but **inside, I was filled with fear.** I tried to suppress the thoughts of, *What will happen* **if** *they find the JESUS film, or the Christian literature translated into Romanian.* "Oh God, help us."

The guard finished looking through all the suitcases. Slowly, he walked to the back of the car and motioned for me to open the trunk. As it rose, the guard stepped forward. I stepped back. He began moving the boxes of juice and food to look below. Silently I groaned, "Oh God, have him stop. Blind his eyes, please Lord." Then he noticed the movie projector on the right side of the trunk. He did not know how to speak English, so he began asking me questions in other languages, French, maybe Italian. I shrugged in ignorance. Finally, he said something which I interpreted as "photographic equipment." I knew that truly understanding each other was an impossibility. Not knowing what to say, I replied, "Sort of." With that he grunted and slammed the trunk shut. Silently I yelled, "Oh God, thank You!"

He began to walk towards the front of the car, but then he stopped. Turning towards me he said something that sounded like "Haben sie Wideo?"

I thought he was asking if we had a radio. Since videos had only become popular in the USA recently, I never dreamed he would know about them. Thus I responded, "Yes, there is one in the car, and we have a big one." I called into the car and asked the girls to show him the boom box (a larger and louder radio than normal).

Irritated, he barked, "Nu, Haben sie Wideo?"

I was totally perplexed. I said, "I just showed you our radios, that's all of them."

In anger, he came to within a foot of me, and yelled, "Haben sie Wideo?"

Filled with fear, I couldn't think straight. Then, from inside the car, Mom and eleven-year-old Michelle yelled, "I think he means a video."

I said, "Oh, no, we don't have any videos."

Disgusted, he motioned for me to put the suitcases back on the rooftop. As I finished getting the suitcases secured on the roof, he returned with our passports stamped with the Romanian visas.

I opened the door, got into the car, drove away, and burst into a prayer, "Oh God, thank You for Your protection. Thank You for stopping him from digging deeper in the trunk. Thank You for not having the movie projector be a problem. Thank You for Mom and Michelle figuring out that he was asking about videos. Thank You, God!"

My shirt was soaked with perspiration. My spirit was filled with joy. I experienced an unforgettable sense of relief. We had made it through the border crossing!

That morning initiated weeks of unanticipated, sometimes frightening situations. Little did we know that in less than twenty-four hours from the border crossing, circumstances would evolve where the potential for interrogation, detainment, and/or prison far exceeded what we experienced at the border.

But I think we may have gotten ahead of ourselves.

The journey that God had for your Grandmom and me didn't start with this first trip to Romania in 1986. There were many amazing, funny, and sometimes miraculous stories that occurred before Romania that we can't let you miss out on hearing. The way God worked in our lives prior to Romania will reveal how creative God can be, **how amazing He is**. So let's go back to the beginning.

Chapter 2

THE JOURNEY BEGINS FOR GRANDDAD

———————⚭———————

From the age of five until I was about ten years old, every night I woke up with the same terrifying dream. At times, I would shake and sweat I was so scared. It was because of those terrifying nightmares that I believe your Nana (my mom) came into my room each night before I went to sleep, and sang a song about Jesus being with me. The words I remember were, "Walking with Jesus, He's right by your side, never to leave you, till morning is nigh," or something like that. I never reasoned that if Jesus was with me, I could trust Him to be with me through the night and the nightmares. But hearing that song every night did cause me to want to know Jesus.

As I grew into my teen years, I continued to think of God in a positive way. Unfortunately, I never truly grasped the Good News of Jesus being my Savior or of the significant relationship I could have with Him. All I heard was, God is loving and therefore you should be a good person.

In college, I went to church a few times during my freshman year, but what I looked forward to the most were the dances and parties on the weekends. It wasn't until my second year in college that things really began to change in my life.

As my sophomore (second) year at Susquehanna University began, I was assigned to live in a different dorm. One night, I met a new guy on the hall and he invited me into his room to get to know him. As we talked, at one point he turned the conversation to God and said that he was an atheist. He told me all the reasons why he didn't believe in God, and then said, "Well you're a theist (someone who believes in God), why do you believe in God?"

I had to win the discussion, so I immediately began to share every reason I could think of for believing in God. The problem was, with each comment I made, I immediately knew one of two things was true. The first thing that could be true was, I was simply making up a reason to believe in God while not really believing it myself. Or second, I was giving a reason I believed, but immediately realized I didn't have a solid intellectual foundation for believing it.

I never let this guy know it, but that night I walked back to my room asking myself, "Why **do** I believe in God?"

Within days, I came to a surprising conclusion as several realizations settled in my mind.

The first realization was that the only real reason I believed in God was because ever since I had been a child, I had been told there was a God. Since my first day in college I had repeatedly heard, "Just because you are told something, that isn't a good reason to believe it." As a result, I began to look back over my life for reasons why I should believe in God.

As I reflected on the first nineteen years of my life, there was only one incident I might describe as a "God intervention-supernatural-unusual moment/event." One event in nineteen years! To me, that single event didn't provide a solid basis for justifying God's existence.

Second, I remembered seeing a banner in church saying, "God is Love." Unfortunately, as I thought about it, I concluded that I had never experienced any of God's love, if He did exist.

Finally, I began to compare knowing God to knowing the President of the United States in a close and personal way. I reasoned that if I knew the President of the United States as a personal friend, whereby he said, "Ron, I really like you. If you ever have a problem, please give me a call. I will see what I can do for you," life would be different.

Having a relationship with the President like that should make my life a lot better than the average Joe American. What situation couldn't be helped by having the President use his power and influence to change circumstances in a positive way? I similarly reasoned, if my life would be different because I knew the President, it should be even more different if I knew the Creator of the universe in a personal way. Unfortunately, apart from spending time in church on a few Sunday mornings and putting as little as possible in the collection plate, I couldn't identify anything that would set my life apart from the humanitarian atheist down the hall.

As a result, the shocking conclusion I made was: *If the God of the Bible existed, I did not know Him.* However, it made logical sense to me that if I could know Him that would be a good thing.

These thoughts propelled me into a four-month search to know God. I asked every person I knew who went to church, "Can you tell me why you believe in God?" Unfortunately, I couldn't find anyone who could give me a convincing answer. Everyone, it seemed, simply said, "Hmmm, I don't know. My parents took me to church, and so I guess I believe in God," or something like that. The more I heard this said, the more frustrated I became with a belief in God. Finally, as the second semester began, I went to see the university chaplain to finally get what I hoped would be an intelligent answer.

As I asked the chaplain for good reasons why I should believe in God, he said in a deep, calm, stately voice, "Oh yes. I believe in God. In the Bible one can find admonitions on how to live life. As I have sought to follow those teachings, I believe that I have become

9

a better person. And as I have encouraged others to do likewise, they have become better people. As a result, I believe that this is a much better world and so yes, I believe in God."

I walked out of the chaplain's office so angry, frustrated, and enraged, that I could have hit someone. Fortunately, since no one was there, I didn't! From that moment forward, to me, Christianity was nothing more than a fairy tale. At best, it was humanitarianism with a mindless, meaningless God attached somewhere at the end.

I went through the rest of my sophomore year growing in my animosity (anger) towards Christians and their stupid beliefs. I concluded that there were three reasons why people believe in God. First, many people went through their entire lives like I did the first nineteen years of my life, believing there was a God simply because they were told there was one. Second, even if God didn't exist, the thought of His existence provided a good escape mechanism for personal inadequacies and failures. People could say, "It's not my fault that I failed, it must be God's will," in order to displace the blame for their own shortcomings. I cannot now remember my third reason why people believed in God, but whatever it was, it only heightened and strengthened my conviction that God did not exist. He only existed in the minds of weak, foolish, non-thinking individuals.

Chapter 3

FROM FRUSTRATION AND ANGER
TO A NEW BEGINNING

—————————∝—————————

During the summer following my sophomore year in college, every weekend that I could I went down to the beach in Ocean City, NJ, to have a good time and possibly meet some girls. One Saturday I had to work till noon and none of my friends were able to go with me, so I simply went alone.

I went to the 9th Street beach where all the college kids hung out, sat down on a bench on the boardwalk, and looked out over the beach to see if there were any girls I might be able to meet and get to know. Within fifteen seconds of sitting down, a couple guys walked up to me and asked if I would mind giving my opinion to a religious survey and something called the Four Spiritual Laws. I never minded giving other people my opinion, so I said yes. Little intrigue was caused by the survey, but then they began going through the Four Spiritual Laws, which begins, "God loves you and offers a wonderful plan for your life."

As they read that, with a sarcastic chuckle I asked them, "Can we be honest in this conversation?"

They responded, "Sure that is what this is all about."

I said "Okay, would you agree with me that you can no more prove the existence of God than I can prove how many gallons of water are out there in that ocean in front of us? I can't prove how many gallons are out there, and you can't prove God's existence, can you? Thus, this whole idea of God is highly suspect, right? Then you say, He is loving. Just so you know where I am coming from, I have heard a lot of fairy tales in my life, and I believe that this is one of the biggest farces out there. But then you say He offers a wonderful plan for your life. How there could ever be a God who is loving and yet have this world be so messed up, I just don't get it. But let's go on." Sarcasm and anger filled every word expressed.

(You might be thinking, "Is that my Granddad? Was my Granddad really like that? Unfortunately, I have to say yes, at that time I was.)

Normally, sharing the truths expressed in the Four Spiritual Laws takes twenty to thirty minutes. That afternoon, due to all my objections, it took two hours. As we finished, I recognized that these two guys were the first people I had ever met who I felt approached their faith in God somewhat intelligently. I didn't agree with all that they said in response to my comments against Christianity, but they had thought about things and made some good points. As we ended our discussion, they told me about a meeting other college students would be at that night at 7pm where the existence of God would be discussed, and invited me to come. I said thanks, but told them I doubted I would come. As they left the boardwalk, I looked out over the beach, intending now to find some girls. Unfortunately, it was now 4pm, and all the college students had left the beach for the day. There were no girls to meet. Bummer!

I wandered on the boardwalk, got something to eat, but knew it would probably be 8pm before I could meet other college students to do something together. Bored out of my mind, I thought, *Why don't you go to that meeting? You can have some fun giving the Christians a hard time about their faith, and maybe set some of them straight. Besides, you have nothing else to do till 8pm.* With this in mind, I went to the hotel and climbed the steps to the second floor. As I reached the top of the stairs, I said to myself, *Ah, you don't want to go in there with those Christians!* I turned around and began going down the steps. But halfway down the steps, again talking to myself, I said, *But what are you going to do for the next hour, walk around bored? Go in there and have some fun.* Thus, I turned around and once again climbed the steps to the second floor.

Looking at the entryway into the meeting room, the thought re-emerged, *Ah, but you don't want to go talk to those 'religious people.'* As I began to turn, to again go down the stairs, my eyes were on the doorway into the room. In God's sovereignty, and possibly with a bit of humor, at that very moment a cute blonde-haired girl walked by inside the room. Continuing with my previous decision, I went halfway down the stairs, but as I thought about that cute girl, I thought, *Maybe this will work out.* I climbed the steps once again to the second floor and entered the room. My eyes immediately went in the direction the girl had walked. To my dismay, she was talking to some guy. I began to leave, but stopped as two students walked up to me and began talking with me. Before I knew it, the meeting began and I thought, *I'll just stay and listen to what they have to say.*

Once again, in God's sovereign plan, the one talk that could have shaken my antagonism towards Christianity and provide a significant reason to reconsider the Christian faith was given that night. The talk was on the historical evidence for the resurrection of Jesus Christ. I was shocked as I heard the explanation surrounding the death and apparent resurrection of Jesus. More upsetting was the claim He made concerning His life that no other sane man in history had ever made. He claimed that He was not just a prophet or philosopher, but that He eternally pre-existed as God the Son, that He had come to earth to reveal the truth about man's existence now and forever, to die to pay the penalty for man's sin, and then He promised He would resurrect from the dead to prove what He said was true.

I was not about to be convinced about anything by a forty-five-minute talk, but the significance of it, if it were true, meant I had to change my entire philosophy and direction in life. Over the next week, I struggled with what had been said, and finally convinced myself that the only reason why it seemed reasonably true was because I hadn't sufficiently examined the arguments. Thus, I went back the next weekend, determined to spend all my time with "those Christian students." I planned to do two things. First, I would observe their lives and see their hypocrisy. This would enable me to ignore all the talk about changed lives and experiencing God's love. Second, I would buy the books they recommended, read them, and rip their weak arguments to shreds.

The next weekend, much to my dismay, the Christian students seemed authentic, admitted that they weren't perfect, and explained that was exactly why they needed a Savior. They wanted to be more Christ-like, but to do so, they needed God's Spirit within them to see inner transformation. I tried to put them down, but they seemed unaffected, while continuing to express acceptance towards me. That Saturday night, I was again shaken by the by the talk that was presented. This time it was, "The probability of one man fulfilling eight of the sixty major prophecies concerning the Messiah coming as the Suffering Servant." As the meeting concluded, I reasoned, *Wow, these guys have thought about their beliefs and why they believe them. I have never heard anything like this.*

As I left the meeting that night, I bought a couple of the books they recommended. I was still fully committed to discrediting their arguments. As I read the books, I didn't agree with every point discussed, but gradually the truths of Christianity began to make more sense. Week after week, I continued to spend every weekend with the Christian students and read every book they recommended. The accumulating evidence led me to conclude that the probability was, Jesus was indeed who He said He was: God in the flesh, revealing the truths for life now and for all eternity, who came to live and die to pay the penalty for my sins. And then He rose from the dead, verifying the truth of His claims.

Unfortunately, although this was where all the evidence pointed, intellectually I was still stuck. Why?

Because I knew that just because something was probable, even overwhelmingly probable, didn't make it true. I wrestled and wrestled with this apparent impasse. Finally, one Saturday night, I got alone on the beach around 1am. Sitting there, looking at the ocean and stars, I finally said, "Jesus, I don't know if You are alive, and if at this very moment You can hear my voice, or if I am like some idiot out here talking to the air. One of the two is true. But, if You are alive, if You can hear my voice right now, I ask You to reveal Yourself to me, to come into my life, to be my Savior because I certainly need one, and to begin doing all the things You said You would. But if You don't, I have had it with this Christianity!"

At that moment, my overwhelming sense of reality was that Jesus was alive. I felt His love surround me for the first time in my life. I was amazed at His presence, existence, and the truth that Jesus was indeed alive from the dead. Creator, Savior, and LORD.

Chapter 4

"There is No God. It's All a Lie!"

———————⟨✕⟩———————

" There is no God. There is no God. It's all a lie!"
"There is no God. There is no God. It's all a lie!"
That's **all** I could hear. "There is no God. There is no God.
There is no God. It's all a lie!"

What was happening? God had revealed the truth of His existence to me on the beach that Saturday night, but now, all I could hear in my mind was that it was all a lie.

A **battle** was raging! Satan (whom Jesus said existed) did not want this new truth of His resurrection and existence to settle in my heart.

As the "It's all a lie" thoughts filled my mind, I fought back with what God had done in my life. I would think through, week by week, how I had gradually gained knowledge and came to believe. From the first conversation on the beach, to the talk on the evidence for the resurrection of Christ, to the probability of one man fulfilling eight of the sixty major prophecies about the suffering Messiah, to the books I read, to the night on the beach when I was overwhelmed with the reality of the **living** God.

At first, thinking through the sequence of events one time cleared my mind. But as the "lie" attacks continued to bombard me, it took two, three, four or more times of mentally going through what had occurred to release me from the mental attack. After a week or two of this battle, I began to be concerned. Deliverance was taking longer and longer before my heart and mind found rest. Soon I would be returning to college, my fraternity house, and the fact that I had not been able to find one true follower of Christ in four months of looking the previous year. How could I survive? How could I make it if these mental battles continued? Back at school, I wouldn't have the time to get my mind back to a sound place of belief.

Troubled and unsettled I prayed, "God, You know I want to follow You and believe in You, but I just can't continue if You don't do something. I can't make it alone, back at school, in the fraternity, battling this way."

For more than a week, I prayed this to God, but there was no change. Frequently throughout the week, "There is no God. There is no God. It's all a lie!" was all I could hear. As the day to leave for college drew near, I continued to pray, but felt weaker and weaker in the fight. I began to doubt that my faith would survive.

And then it happened.

In the book of Job, chapter 1, verse 10, Satan complains to God regarding Job and says, "Have You not made a hedge about him and his house and all that he has, on every side? You have blessed the work of his hands, and his possessions have increased in the land. But put forth Your hand now and touch all that he has; he will surely curse You to Your face." God had blessed Job and placed a hedge of protection around him.

I cannot remember the moment, or even how it occurred, but what I know is that just before I returned to college, the presence and reality that God was real became my experience and reality from the moment I woke in the morning, till the moment I went to sleep at night. The mental battle saying, "There is no God. There is no God. It's all a lie!" vanished.

17

For the next six months, the presence of God and His love for me was so real, so true, and so apparent, the only way I can describe it is, "God put a hedge around me." It seems that what God removed from Job, He placed around me.

As I enjoyed God's love and presence over the following months, I continually looked forward to the time each day when I could read His word, and gradually grow in the knowledge of Him and His truths. It was a wonderful and tremendous period of growth in the Lord.

But, then **something happened**!

I can vividly recall one day walking across campus, when all of a sudden my awareness of God's presence was gone. I looked for the feeling of His presence, the sense of His love. Nothing. It was as if God never existed. I felt alone, that I was all by myself. If God did exist, He was somewhere out there in space, millions and millions of miles away. Had I just convinced myself that God was real? Was the "true reality," that there is no God, finally breaking though my fantasy world?

Perplexed, I began to wrestle in my mind. Immediately, the thought, "There is no God. There is no God. It's all a lie!" returned. The battle for my mind had reemerged. The hedge had been removed.

However, by this time, I had learned from the Word of God that I could not stand on my emotions. Rather, I needed to stand on the truth revealed in God's Word. My mind went to Genesis 1:1, "In the beginning God created the heavens and the earth." And truths from John 1:1-3, "In the beginning was the Word, and the Word was with God, and the Word was God. He was in the beginning with God. All things came into being through Him, and apart from Him nothing came into being that has come into being." John 14:6, "I am the Way, the Truth, and the Life," and many other verses filled my mind.

I began to see and understand another truth in my life. I began to see the truth and power of God's Word destroy the power of the lies of our enemy, the devil. Victory began to be mine. Not because I felt the presence of God, but because I began to stand on the truth of His Word.

Chapter 5

GRANDMOM'S STORY

———————⟨×⟩———————

L et me take you back to my sophomore year in college...
Although I had been religious growing up and was the only
one in my family to go to church (except on Easter and sometimes
Christmas Eve), let alone be involved in all the Sunday school,
youth group, choir, Vacation Bible School, and summer camp activities possible, it wasn't until second semester, sophomore year in
college that I understood for the first time what it was to have a
personal relationship with God through Christ.

When I went off to college, I left the familiarities and secu-
rities of having grown up in a small town, and went to a very
large university, in a large city. It was an adjustment, for sure. It
was a long year, full of difficult roommate situations and studying,
studying, studying! By the time I returned for my second year, I
was more determined than ever to make more of my college experience. There had to be more. Basically, for me that meant being
involved in more activities, more clubs and hopefully carving out
more time from studies to meet and make more friends. Sounds
like I felt like "more" would make things better, doesn't it? True
enough. One of my favorite "mores" was Judo Club, where I actually learned how to quickly throw big, heavy guys to the ground in
seconds. They never seemed to think I could, but they were quickly

proven wrong. I was amazed at how powerful a simple move actually could be, and I will admit that it was fun to amaze my friends **and** to have some power!

It was fun and certainly better in many ways than my first year at the university, but it didn't take long for me to have a vague sense that, even with all the new experiences, friends, and involvement, something was missing. I just couldn't put my finger on it.

About this time, Janet, a good friend from my freshmen year who sang in the university chorale with me, began to ask me questions about some Christian materials someone had given her. In her mind, since I wasn't Jewish, I was Christian. Of course, since I had always been involved in church, I would have agreed with her on that point, but I really didn't want to discuss it with her. Janet, on the other hand, had grown up Jewish and she was trying to understand how Jesus fit into the picture, if He even did.

Through the next few months, it was obvious to me that something had changed with Janet. She was different: more outgoing, happier, more free, it seemed. When I asked her what was going on, she began to share with me how she had done a lot of reading and searching and realized that Jesus was the Messiah for the Jewish people. She had given her life to Yeshua as her Messiah, Savior and Lord. What? I had no idea what she was talking about!

Janet introduced me to Nan, a staff gal with Cru, who invited me to a special meeting where the speaker talked about the book of Revelation in the Bible and the end times. After the talk, I could not speak, literally. Not at all, except to say, "I can't talk," for almost twenty-four hours because I was so amazed, confused, and overwhelmed from the message. How strange! A few days afterward, I met with Janet and Nan, who shared the Gospel message with me. My years in Sunday school and church had taught me about God's love, somewhat about man's sin, and certainly about Jesus' sacrificial death on the cross for man's rebellion. The missing, significant puzzle piece was that God wanted to have a personal relationship with me through Jesus, and that, even though it was offered to me as a free gift, I needed to accept that gift as I understood my need for His death in light of my own sin.

After I became a true Christian (Christ in one — Christ in **me**!), my life **really** changed! The problem, though, was that I went from being basically easygoing and relatively happy with my life, to being extremely frustrated and in turmoil. Surprised? Bet that's **not** what you **expected** me to say!

To help you understand the problem, let me take you back even farther in my life for a little bit, and give you a glimpse into my high school years. You name it and I was probably involved in it, or something similar: Academics, sports, clubs, leadership, editor of the school newspaper, musicals, speech competition teams. I loved being involved, making a difference, being challenged, and excelling.

Philosophies of life are stated and get played out in different ways in peoples' lives. A speech I gave at my high school graduation was summed up in this quote: "Life is what you make it, so take it, and make it beautiful!" That was how I approached life — approached everything I did. When you are able to do almost anything you want to do, give it all you've got and excel, things can be pretty good, right?

So, let's scroll ahead again to my sophomore year…becoming a true Christian, reading my Bible, studying the Bible, in Bible studies with others, and trying to live the way I thought the words in the Bible were telling me to live. **But** I fell sooooo short. Even though I was a "pretty good person" by the world's standards, I just couldn't seem to "**do**" or "**be**" everything I thought God wanted.

Here's an example of what I mean: I remember being in a Bible study with others, reading through 1 Corinthians 13. This is a passage that speaks of what constitutes real love. Now I was viewing a lengthy relationship with a guy back home through a different grid and trying to make some sense out of it…trying to make the relationship look and work like the love passage in 1 Corinthians 13. But, whether it was the relationship, or anything else in my life, it seemed there was a big gap between what I wanted to do, in light of what I saw in the Bible, and what I was actually able to do with measurable success or excellence. My philosophy of life was no longer working — I couldn't make things work.

Put it together, shake it up, and what do you have? **Frustration, anxiety**, and even fists pounded into the wall! Who was this person? It truly was a little scary to look in the mirror and see this "new person" now that I had become a true Christian. About this same time, I began having some serious physical symptoms, though I wasn't aware of the connection to my frustrations at the time. The physical symptoms became such a concern that I ended up in the emergency room in the city where I went to the university. Not long afterward I was sent home for special testing, and ultimately to a special medical facility out of state where the diagnosis was that they couldn't figure out the problem. Now, there's a "diagnosis" if ever there was one! Oh, and by-the-way, I would need to take medication for the rest of my life to control the problems (losing my hearing, and some pretty serious GI problems). Not such good news for me or for my parents.

It reminds me of the struggle the apostle Paul refers to in Romans 7:15, 18b, 19:

> "I do not understand my own actions. For I do not do
> what I want, but I do the very thing I hate
> …For I have the desire to do what is right, but not
> the ability to carry it out.
> For I do not do the good I want, but the evil I do not
> want is what I keep on doing." (ESV)

I was not the same person and it was frustrating and confusing, to say the least.

Classes had ended. I was back home and had just gotten the news from the out-of-state specialist that I would need to take pills for, most likely, the rest of my life. The pill bottle had been stared at plenty in passing, as it sat, still unopened, on my bedroom dresser. Maybe I was still somewhat in shock at the whole situation. Maybe it was just procrastination. Maybe…

Then the call came from the Cru staff from my university, inviting me to a two-week conference in Ocean City, NJ. I was in western New York state, a bit of a trip from the ocean, but they said they could stop by my home, pick me up and bring me back after the conference was over. There would be hundreds of college students from all over the US there, with great speakers, training, fun and worship. It was **good** news after the recent bad news. Though my parents were reluctant at first to let me go away for two weeks so soon after all the health escapades, I guess maybe they saw how my whole demeanor changed with the possibility, and they finally said "yes"!

Hang in there with me now. This is where things get even more interesting, and quite amazing.

Day One:

On the first full day, after all the great morning speakers and seminars, everyone had the opportunity to practice sharing the Gospel message with one other person at the meeting. After a quick lunch, we were on the beach, taking surveys, as I recall, and trying to engage in spiritual conversations with anyone who might be even slightly interested. I would not be exaggerating to say it was one of the most difficult days of my life, at least when it would come to my peers. Not one person was interested, even in the slightest. In fact, they were quite rude and antagonistic. It was pretty awful.

That night, sitting close to the front so I could hear (remember, I was suffering from extensive hearing loss as one of my mysterious health symptoms), there was an opportunity for people to share stories from their day on the beach, talking to other students about Jesus. Crazy stories! Amazing stories! Stories of people asking deep questions and people responding to the truths of God's Word. I was struggling, trying to understand the sharp contrast between my experience that day and all the wonderful experiences others had had. Why was life so much the worse for me as a Christian — both as I listened to their experiences in sharing their faith, and, as I thought of my life **before** I gave my life to Christ?

Day Two:

Again, the morning was filled with great speakers, seminars and wonderful worship. Again, I was sitting close to the front to hear. Again, we practiced sharing with one other person before going out to the beach. Only this time, the small booklet was for anyone we might meet who was a believer. It was a book about God's Holy Spirit within the believer and God's purpose and ministry in giving us His Holy Spirit.

This was the first time I ever remember hearing anything about the Holy Spirit (except as part of the Trinity). I was listening hard! So hard...right then and there, in the "practice time", my heart was responding to the need to let go and let God be the One in control, through His Holy Spirit that now lived inside me as a child of God. You can only begin to imagine the **huge, huge** burden that was lifted from my life. I no longer had to try to live the Christian life in my own strength, but God had provided the power within me as His child so that I could live that life. Believe me when I say how powerful, real and freeing this was for me...all in a matter of minutes. And my life would never, never be the same. God was about to give me an incredible lesson I would never forget.

That day I stepped off the boardwalk into the sand, hoping someone would be interested in some level of a spiritual conversation. It was the same spot I had stepped off the day before: the

Ocean City 9th Street boardwalk entrance to the beach. Only God knew what would happen from that point forward. Only God knew, because He already had everything in place for me, for my lesson!

It was tempting, especially after the day before, to bypass the blanket of girls within eight feet of the stairs, but I chose to stop and for the next one-and-a-half hours they engaged in spiritual conversation with me, asking tons of questions, and they were genuinely interested in hearing about Jesus. It was definitely a God thing! As I was picking up my things to leave, a girl from a group nearby jumped up, came over and said something to me like, "We overheard you talking to them about God. Can you come talk to us about God?" And so the afternoon continued without me moving more than three blankets away from the 9th Street entrance to the beach!

Getting to the meeting late that night, my friends and I had to sit near the back. And there I was, so excited about what God had done that day, suddenly shocked as I realized I was sitting near the back, and I could **hear**! Clear as a bell. Loud and clear. And there is something else I haven't told you yet. Though some might say I wasn't being a very good patient, the fact remains that I had not yet taken even one pill that the specialist had prescribed! From that point forward, not only did I never ever take one of those pills, I never had to! All my mysterious symptoms were gone. No kidding! God did an amazing thing for me in that one day. He showed me His truth. He showed me a sharp, sharp contrast between doing things in my own "power" and walking in His power through surrendering control to His Holy Spirit. The lesson was dramatic, without a doubt, but I am convinced in His perfect wisdom and plan, He knew me so, so well and knew I needed to clearly and unmistakably see how fruitless and how destructive it can be to live life trying to be the one in control. And He needed to show me clearly and unmistakably how freeing and powerful it can be to live surrendered to Him and His power within us.

Though the message was loud and clear, and the heart to surrender was as sincere as anything ever could be, the surrendered life isn't a once-and-done deal. It is a daily choice. Sometimes it can feel like it is a moment-to-moment choice to let God be in control of my life — to give up the trying, trying, trying to "**be**" or to "**do**". Who better to be in control, when you stop and think about it, than the One who created us, knows us better than we know ourselves, and the One who loves us completely! He has set us free and has given us His Spirit within us.

Romans 8:11 talks about this: "But if the Spirit of Him who raised Jesus from the dead dwells in you, He who raised Christ Jesus from the dead will also give life to your mortal bodies through His Spirit who dwells in you." Did you catch that? The same Spirit of Him who raised Jesus from the dead is the Spirit that lives in us as believers in Jesus! Wow! Now, that is a whole lot of power!

Chapter 6

GRANDMOM: AN AMAZING STORY OF LOVE FROM ABOVE, MRS. B

———————∝———————

I t was the summer of 1971, between my third (junior) and fourth (senior) year of college. There was lots of excitement in being at "the shore" in Ocean City, NJ, for most of the summer. There was my job, working at a bandage factory (summer jobs often add perspective to even the young, and a respect for those who work day in and day out doing the tedious and mundane, year after year, often because there is no other choice). There were over 100 college students from all over the country, myself one of them, all of whom had jobs for the summer but were involved in a ministry leadership development project together during off hours.

Well, that was why I was so far from home for the summer, but now to **this** story...

There was no email those days, and phone calls were too costly to be taken lightly, so letters were my touch point with home. Mom wrote often. Early on in the summer, Mom added something at the end of her letter that truly was the beginning of an amazing tapestry being woven to show how great God's love is, and how His love and grace pursue beyond all we could ever ask or imagine.

The letter mentioned that Mrs. B was very ill with cancer, and the prognosis was not good. That comment stirred an emotional connection from years gone by. My family had vacationed at a nearby lake for several summers and had met Mrs. B and her family who were always there the same weeks. They also lived just eight miles from our town. Her son, Albert, became an early high school sweetheart for me. But years had passed, and those days were but memories of another time. Something else had sprung to life with those words. I think it was something about Mrs. B herself that is difficult to describe, or maybe it was God's heart stirring my own. I had especially liked her, and she seemed like such a dear woman, a caring mother, and she was always sweet and tender toward me. At least, that was how I remembered her. Somehow she was, even though briefly in my life, special to me.

She had impressed me from the beginning with her strong commitment to her Catholic faith. It seemed important to her and her desires for the family she cared for and loved. Soon after one of those early letters from home, my heart was pounding and I couldn't set aside the compelling desire—no—*need*, to go and see her as soon as I ended my summer commitment to the project, before returning to the university.

With each letter from home, there were lines penned about Mrs. B. Apparently the doctors didn't expect her to make it through the summer. My heart somehow broke with those words. So here I was, far away, hearing that this dear woman was terribly ill and finding myself drawn to see her. And so, I made a vow to God, that if He would keep her alive until I could get home, I would go to see her. Needless-to-say, as letters continued from home, I always searched first for news of her. And, there were always the added words that went something like, "but everyone is surprised that Mrs. B is still with us."

Most likely, at this point, you are at least a little confused at the compelling nature of my inmost being to *need* to see this woman whom I hadn't seen for years. It was a bit surprising to me as well. Perhaps what I am about to share, before continuing the rest of the story, will provide the answer to that begging question. Hang in here with me as some of my story is retold, yet with some pertinent details, even if you already think you know what I am going to say. Promise?

In the previous chapter, I mentioned how active I had been in church as I was growing up. By anyone's standards, I think one could fairly say I was religious. My heart was sensitive to the things of God. I knew about God's love for us, summed up in John 3:16: "For God so loved the world that He gave His only begotten son, that whoever believes in Him shall not perish but have eternal life."

For years I had heard about the sinfulness of man and understood in some way that my sin separated me from the God who created all things. Because He was God, and perfect, and I was not, that sin kept me from Him. Romans 3:23: "For all have sinned and fall short of the glory of God."

Then, of course, there was Jesus Christ, God in the flesh, who dwelt among us and became the sacrifice for our sins through His death on the cross. It is through Him that we can know God and experience God's love. Romans 5:8: "But God demonstrates His own love for us, in that while we were yet sinners, Christ died for us." And John 14:6: "Jesus said to him, 'I am the way, and the truth and the life; no one comes to the Father, but through Me.'" God had bridged that separation by sending His Son. These truths were part of my life.

Then came college, and for whatever reason, church and God took a backseat in my life.

At the same time, the "life is what you make it, so take it and make it beautiful" philosophy that had permeated my high school days and the plethora of activities was a far cry from my college experience my freshman year. So my determination, as I went back for my second year in college, was fortified to fill in the gaps. I got involved in different activities, even getting my yellow belt in Judo (and yes, I really could throw big, strong men!). But still, there was something that wasn't right, like that "missing piece of the puzzle" that can drive some of us crazy.

About that time, a good friend shared something with me that rattled my categories. It was something I had never heard before and certainly never understood. The missing puzzle piece...to my life. Yes, it was essential for me to understand and believe the other three tenets of the faith, but to know God personally and experience His love, it was, by God's design, a choice I would have to make to individually receive Christ as my Savior and Lord. It really was two things that come again, from the Scriptures. The gospel of John, chapter 1, verse 12, was the first to grab my attention. It says, "But as many as received Him, to them He gave the right to become children of God, even to those who believe in His name." The second comes from Ephesians 2:8,9: "For by grace you have been saved through faith; and that not of yourselves, it is the gift of God; not as a result of works, so that no one may boast."

She likened it to a gift, in the truest sense of the word — freely given, but not really ours, even though our name might be on the tag, until we open it and take it as our own. Offered but not ours to experience until we receive it. And, there is nothing we can **do** — to get it, to deserve it, to be worthy — it is God's **gift**. Christ is speaking in Revelation 3:20 and says, "Behold, I stand at the door and knock; if anyone hears My voice and opens the door, I will come in to him..." I needed to open the door of my life and receive, personally, the gift God was offering through Jesus — the forgiveness of sins — past, present and future, a personal relationship with Him, and the promise of eternity with Him. It was undeniably a point of transformation in my life — and freedom from a form of "church-ianity" to a relationship with the living God.

Now let me continue the story . . .

The project ended and I was home for about a week, preparing to return for my senior year. Honestly, I was terrified in a way to call and visit Mrs. B. It had been at least five years since I had seen the family. I was young, Mrs. B was very religious, and I didn't in any way want to be presumptuous as I hoped to share with her the truths I just mentioned above, and sadly, she was dying. And so, I procrastinated until the day before I had to leave for school.

As I remember it, I called and just asked if I could come by and visit, and must not have mentioned wanting to see her, specifically. I'm sure the daughters, then grown, must have been baffled by the request, but they welcomed me. After some time chatting in the living room, I asked if I could go in to see their mother. They looked at each other, then back at me. Their words hung on my heart like a millstone: "She's not here. She's been transferred to another hospital." When they said where, the lump in my throat got even bigger. Buffalo. You probably didn't know, but I went to the University of Buffalo. It seemed undeniable that God wanted me to continue to pursue Him on this journey and meet with Mrs. B, in Buffalo!

My friend, Dan, drove me to the hospital shortly after I got settled back in the dorms, and we prayed together before I went to the hospital room. The room was "filled" with family who were unfamiliar to me, and nurses. Mrs. B clutched my hand and knew who I was, but was in obvious pain and couldn't focus for long, until the nurse gave her a shot. Then she was no longer in pain, but she also was even less coherent as a result. All the circumstances made it impossible to share what was on my heart with her. It's hard to explain how overwhelmed, sad, and perplexed I felt as I walked out, almost in a daze, not understanding what had just happened in light of what seemed to be something God had put on my heart. When I got back in the car with my friend, and explained all that had happened, we prayed together. Without missing a beat, he lovingly, but insistently said, "You need to go back."

A few days later, Dan drove me once again to the hospital. This time we sat in the parking lot at length and prayed some very bold and very specific prayers. If God had truly been a part of the process in my life related to Mrs. B the past months, then we prayed: 1) that there would be no medical personnel in the room; 2) no family or friends in the room; 3) that she would be free of pain; and 4) that she would be coherent and able to fully focus — all for as long as it would take for me to say whatever it was that God wanted her to hear through my words that day.

And to my utter amazement, every one of those things was true — for as long as I was in the room with her! The whole scenario in the room was in sharp contrast to what it had been just days before. Does God **always** respond to our specific prayers with such a resounding "**yes**"? No, He does not, basically because it is all about God and not about me. But that day, God had most definitely put those specifics on my heart, and He was in control.

And then, after some time, I got to share those truths from God's Word that I have written in the paragraphs above — piece by piece, verse by verse. I told her I knew she was a religious woman and her Catholic faith was important to her. I briefly told her my story of being religious and trying to do what was "right", and yet discovering it was about putting my faith, my trust in Christ alone as my Savior. I then shared the words of a prayer with her that went something like this: "Lord Jesus, I want to be sure I know You personally. Thank You for dying on the cross for me — for my sins. I open the door of my life and receive You as Savior and Lord. Thank You for forgiving my sins and giving me eternal life. With the days I have left, take control of the throne of my life." I have never forgotten, and remember with tears in my eyes even now, how tightly she clutched my hands, with tears flooding her eyes and beginning to stream down her face, as she asked me to please pray the prayer out loud for her because she was too weak. And I did. I knelt beside her hospital bed and prayed. She nodded her head in agreement ever so slightly. Her tears were smothered by her fresh smile and a "thank you" that was full of peace. At that moment, I felt she grasped her need to place her faith in Jesus alone as her Savior. It was an unforgettable moment and I am humbled at how powerfully and specifically God answered prayers that day — not just our prayers in the parking lot, but, I believe, the prayers of a woman's heart to be sure of her eternal destiny and God's love and forgiveness.

Several days later, I called the hospital before planning to visit. Mrs. B had left this earth, but I know she was rejoicing in her new heavenly home.

Obviously, many, many years have since passed, but the picture is so, so clear to me —like it was just yesterday. Yes, the picture and words and all that tangibly transpired. But more than that, the beautiful picture of God's amazing love that would go to such lengths for one person to know for certain she was His own: forgiven, loved and assured of eternity with Him

Chapter 7

THE GREATEST IDEA EVER!

———————∝———————

I t was around midnight in January, about six months after I began
following Christ. I was in bed on the top bunk in my fraternity
room, looking at the ceiling. For some reason, my thoughts jumped
into the future, thinking about the summer. Within seconds, the
greatest idea ever began to formulate in my mind.

Thoughts raced, envisioning the adventure it would be to hitchhike across the country that summer. Every day would bring new
situations, circumstances, people, sights of the country, and nev-
er-before-experienced events. Being a Christian, and now knowing
several areas in which God would want me to grow and mature, I
quickly saw how many of them could occur if I was hitchhiking
across the country. How, you might ask? Let me tell you.

First, I knew God wanted me to grow in the intimacy of my
relationship with Him. If I were to hitchhike across the county, in a
sense, every day "was my own", to determine what to do, where to
go, and what to do next. Thus, every day, I could spend as much time
in prayer, reading the Bible, and just being with God as I wanted.

Second, God wants us to grow in the depth of our understanding
of **His** Word. I had heard that at the international headquarters of
Cru, undergrad and graduate level theology and Bible study courses
were offered during the summer. Thus, my plan was to hitchhike

across the country to San Francisco, go down the California coast to San Bernardino to the headquarters of Cru, possibly work on the grounds to make some money, and take one of the courses they offered.

Third, I knew God wanted me to share with others how fantastic it was to know **Him**. Doing this would be one of the simplest things to do as a hitchhiker. Every time you get picked up, the natural conversation goes to who are you, where are you from, where are you headed, etc. It would be completely natural and easy to share my testimony and about my relationship with Jesus as I shared about my life. I committed right then and there on that top bunk, to share my testimony and the Good News of Jesus with every person who picked me up. Just think of it. Every day, I would probably be picked up by between four and ten people. If it took me twenty days to hitchhike across the country, and it averaged out so seven people picked me up each day, I would have shared with 140 people. How exciting and glorifying to God would that be?

Fourth, I knew God wanted me to grow in my practical faith and dependence upon Him. Thus within minutes as this **greatest idea ever** evolved, I decided to leave for the summer with $25 in my pocket, and trust God to miraculously provide for my needs through people, circumstances, and/or getting one or two day jobs along the way.

Wow! What an adventure! Could there be any better way to walk with God, grow in Him, share Him with others, or grow in my practical everyday faith and dependence upon Him? **No way**, in my estimation. That night I could hardly sleep, thinking about the possibilities.

However, I also knew God was smarter than I was. Right? The answer is **yes**!

Thus, as I reflected on the **greatest idea ever**, I recognized there were a couple other possible ways to spend my summer. The second possibility was to go home, work at the job that I had had since I was sixteen, make a good bit of money, go to the beach on the weekends, and continue my normal summer life. The third possibility was to participate in the Cru Summer Leadership Project in Ocean City, NJ, like the students I had met the previous summer.

One thing I tend to do as I consider various decisions is to rate the possibilities on a scale of 1 to 10, with 10 being the best, and 1 being the least desirable. As I contemplated hitchhiking across the country, without a doubt, it was a 10. Working at home and going to the beach on the weekends was a 5. But being stuck in little Ocean City all summer, even if I was participating with the project, was about a 3.

Each night as I spent time in prayer and thought about the summer, I would say something like, "God, You know that there are three things I can do this summer. And You know how excited I am about hitchhiking across the country. But, You are wiser than I am and I believe You have Your purposes. So I ask You to lead me to what You want me to do — to hitchhike across the country, work at home, or go to OC. I ask in Jesus' name. Amen."

As the months of January, February, and March went by, and as I continued to pray, I sensed a slight shift in my ratings. The exciting passion to hitchhike across the country dropped slightly from a 10 to a 9.5. Staying at home remained a neutral 5. Going to Ocean City remained the lowest, but it did rise a bit to what I would say was a 3.5 or 4.

Spring break came and I headed home to talk about the summer with Nana and FarFar (the names given to my parents later on. Nana was for *grandmother* and FarFar was Swedish for *father's father*). I was trying to get a sense of their openness to options in terms of my summer but purposefully mentioned only two of the three possibilities. Guess which one I omitted?

They were fine with me staying at home, and/or going to Ocean City for the summer. I also talked with my younger sister, your Aunt Renee, who was fifteen, but would turn sixteen in June. When

I was home for Christmas break the previous December, one night I got to share with Renee more about a relationship with Christ, about our need for Him to be our Savior and to guide us in this life. Renee was very responsive, and she placed her faith in Christ that night. Pretty cool, huh? God is so gracious and good!

But unfortunately, as a junior in high school, your Aunt Renee was hanging out with a crowd that was having a very bad influence on her. She knew no other students who were truly walking with the Lord, so it was very hard for her to break away from this group of friends. In one way she wanted to, but she just couldn't find a way to do it. As we continued to talk, my level of concern grew as I understood the depth of the challenges and difficulties she was facing.

One night, I found myself asking my parents, "Renee will turn sixteen in June and will be able to get working papers. If I went to OC this summer, and was willing to look out for her, would you let her come down to the shore with me?" Amazingly, Nana and FarFar said yes. I was convinced that if Renee could get away from her friends for the summer and spend her free time hanging out with all the committed Christian college kids, she would grow in her relationship with Christ. Then maybe she would have the strength and faith to break away from those friends who were having a bad influence on her.

That night, as I prayed to God about my summer, I realized my rating system for the summer had radically changed. Hitchhiking across the country continued to be, and probably would always be a 9 or 9+. Staying at home remained a 5. However, participating in the summer project, and possibly seeing your Aunt Renee's life changed, with the potential of her being able to break away from those friends, transformed going to OC from a 4 to a 10.

Ocean City, here I come!

Chapter 8

GOD HAS A BETTER IDEA

I knew God was smarter than I was (duh!), but I had no way of knowing **all** the life-changing things God had in mind for my summer.

The decision to go to Ocean City occurred on Wednesday night of spring break. Immediately, I knew I needed to get a job in OC for the summer. I decided to drive down on Friday, see if any businesses were open and put in applications for different jobs. I was a bit disappointed with the outcome of my trip. Only a few businesses were open during the off season, and most of those weren't taking applications. I got to submit two or three applications, but when I talked with the owners about actually getting a job, they weren't too encouraging.

As I thought about the summer, I felt acquiring a job was God's problem or responsibility, and my responsibility was to simply continue to follow Him.

About a week after I returned to college from spring break, my roommate, who didn't know the Lord and was strongly opposed to my Christian faith, came into the room. Surprisingly he said, "Hey Ron, aren't you thinking about going to Ocean City this summer?"

I said, "Yeah."

He said, "I was just over at the university employment agency and I saw this flier. Thought you might be interested in it."

Saying thanks, I picked it up and read that a former graduate of Susquehanna University had just purchased a hotel in Ocean City. He was coming that Saturday to give interviews to students from his alma mater so they could spend the summer working in his hotel. Immediately I said, "God, You are so cool! I can't get back to Ocean City before the summer to get a job, so You brought one to me. Amazing!"

That Saturday, I would interview and see God provide me with a job. Or so I thought.

It was Saturday morning at 8:30am. The one telephone on the floor in my fraternity house rang. I awoke to a **very angry** voice **screaming** from down the hall, **"Bystrom**, you have a call at 8:30 on Saturday morning!" I rolled out of my bunk and half-asleep, walked to the telephone. On the phone was the Dean of Students from the university. He was a Christian and I had gotten to know him since I had become a Christian the summer before.

He said, "Ron, I hate to call you this early on a Saturday morning, but I really need your help. Timmy (his three-year-old son) got sick last night. He has a high temperature and was throwing up all night. This morning Viv (his wife Vivian) was going to take me to the airport since I have to fly to St Louis for a conference. Obviously, she can't with Timmy's sickness. I have tried several other people and no one can help me. Is there any way you can drive me to the airport this morning? I need to leave between 9:30-9:45."

Standing there, silently I said, "God, what are You doing? How can I go to the airport and be back in time for the job interview?"

But I couldn't imagine saying no to the Dean of Students, and so I said, "Sure, I'll see you in an hour."

As we went to the airport, my eyes continually went to my watch. The interviews for the jobs in OC were to be given from 10am-1pm. Watching my speed, I got back to school around noon.

As I walked from my car towards the office where the interviews were being taken, I said, "God, I guess You knew You could have me help the Dean *and* get the interview. Thanks for working it out so I could do both."

As I approached the office, I noticed the lights were off. The door was locked and no one was inside. Bewildered, I walked away saying, "God, I don't know what is going on, but I guess You do."

Monday afternoon a week and two days later at about 3pm, something unusual occurred. In the middle of the afternoon, I was trying to study. I had an exam in a couple of days, and I decided to get ahead in preparing for it.

Without warning, suddenly, this crazy thought came to my mind: *Write the owner of the hotel, and ask him for a job.*

I tried to study but the thought came back: *Write the owner of the hotel and ask him for a job.*

Again, I attempted to put the thought out of my mind and study, but the thought would not go away. Finally, I decided, *I am not going to get anything done until I write this guy and ask him for a job.* I pushed my book to the side, took out some paper and began to write a letter. I shared with the owner who I was, told him the jobs I had had since I was sixteen, and expressed to him that I would prefer getting the bell boy job. This entailed carrying bags for people as they arrived or left the hotel, or other favors, for which they would tip me.

Why that job, you might ask? Over the weeks since spring break, I began to calculate how much money I needed to earn that summer to cover my summer costs in OC and save for my college expenses the next year. What I found out was that I needed to cover all my expenses for housing, food, travel, etc., and save $700 for college ($700 would be something like saving $6,000-$7,000 during the summer today). As I looked at all the possible jobs, it appeared I could make the most money by being the bell boy if

I received good tips. My other thought was that if I didn't make enough money with this job, I would just get a second part-time job.

I finished the letter, put in a picture of myself, and planned to mail it that night. Now, I could get back to studying.

A few days later, as I was walking across campus, I met a guy named Dave whom I had known on my floor during my freshman year. We talked and what we were going to do that summer came up. He was so excited. He told me about this grad who bought a hotel in Ocean City who had come to give interviews to students from our school. He said he went, got interviewed, and got the job as the bell boy.

I said, "Oh, that's great. Are you sure you are going to do this?"

He said, "Are you kidding? I've wanted to work down the shore for a summer since I was in high school. There is no way this isn't going to happen."

"What about the other jobs?" I asked. "Do you think there are other job opportunities left?"

He said, "Not a chance. There were seven jobs offered. That morning the office was packed. The owner took about thirty interviews, and was out of there before 11:30. He got more applications than he needed."

Walking away, I said, "God, I don't know what's going on. I guess that wasn't You telling me to write the owner. You know I still need a job. But that is Your responsibility. I am just following."

About a week later, I went to my mailbox at the university. Amazingly, I got something other than junk mail.

I saw a letter from the owner of the hotel. Rather perplexed, I opened the letter and began to read something like this:

Dear Ron:

I received your letter and am happy to inform you that I have decided to give you the job of the bell boy. This is a rather unusual step since I have not met you. I will be at the hotel the two middle weekends in May. Is there a chance you could come one of those weekends to meet me? At that time we can discuss the responsibilities of being the bell boy. Please let me know as soon as possible if you would like the job, and if you can meet me in Ocean City either of those weekends. I hope it works out.

Harold Snyder.

I couldn't believe what I had just read. In fact, I read it again to make sure I got it right. I said, "Wow, God, **You are amazing!**"

It is interesting to me that I never ran into Dave again. I didn't see him during the remaining weeks that spring semester, nor during my entire senior year of college. As a result, I do not know what happened to cause Dave to change his plans. All I know is, something occurred and Dave no longer could do the job.

I checked my final exam schedule and realized that I could go down to Ocean City one of the weekends Mr. Snyder mentioned. I immediately wrote him, thanked him, accepted the job, and told him I could drive down to OC during one of the weekends.

But what you have heard to this point is not the craziest, or the most amazing part of this story.

After I arrived at the hotel a couple weeks later, Mr. Snyder immediately took me on a tour of the hotel, and then we went to the front porch to sit down and discuss the job and its responsibilities.

As we sat down, the first words out of his mouth were, "Well you know why you got this job, don't you?"

Surprised, I responded, "Well, I sent you that letter telling you about me, and shared the job experiences I have had."

He began to chuckle and said, "You don't honestly believe that is why you got the job do you? I had over thirty applications."

I responded, "Well, I don't know what else to say."

Here was his response: "The only reason you got the job is because 'Mrs. Smith' wrote me and asked me to give you the job. (I have no idea what Mrs. Smith's real name is). We graduated together and she works in an office at the university. The day before I received your letter, I received a letter from her in which she raved about you. She asked me if there was any job opportunity that arose, please give it to you. Then just before I opened your letter, I received a letter from the student to whom I had given the bell boy job. He said he could no longer come this summer. Thus, when I read your letter, I immediately wrote you, giving you the job. But it is really because of Mrs. Smith's request that you got the job."

Shocked and hesitant I said, "I am sorry, Mr. Snyder, but I have never met and do not know who Mrs. Smith is."

Now it was Mr. Snyder who was shocked. He never checked the names to be sure I was the student mentioned in Mrs. Smith's letter. When he got my letter, he simply assumed that I was the student about whom Mrs. Smith raved.

Now there was a sudden, awkward moment of silence. We both came to the realization that I was not the person he had intended to hire. Both of us sat there, not knowing what to say.

Finally he said, "Well after you traveled several hours to get here, I can't *not* give you the job." For this I was very grateful. But then another surprise occurred. Mr. Snyder began telling me about the job of the bell boy, the responsibilities, and the amount of tips I could expect to receive. It wasn't good news.

He told me that I would work from 7am to 10am, and then from 3:30pm to 6:30pm, seven days a week. He continued by telling me what my pay would be, and what I could expect to receive from tips. My jaw almost dropped. Doing quick calculations in my mind, I knew immediately there was no way I could save the amount of money I needed to save for that summer with this job. And, with the hours being what they were, I knew it would be virtually impossible to get the second job I had already planned to get if I needed it. No one could get a job working from 11am to 2:30pm at the beach.

I silently thought, *Should I refuse the job?*

I quickly concluded, however, given all that had occurred, this job had to be what God had orchestrated. Somehow, God would have to work it out so that I could make the other money I needed. How? I had no idea. Soon, I would find out that God can use all kinds of circumstances to fulfill His ultimate plan.

*****

There was yelling, fist pounding, confusion, and police.

Apparently, someone had stolen money from the safe at the hotel. Mr. Snyder and others involved in the situation argued about what should happen, while also attempting to keep the specifics of what had occurred from the other staff of the hotel.

I had worked at the hotel as the bell boy for about two weeks and it was near the end of my shift when Mr. Snyder approached me.

He said, "Ron, after you are done with your shift, can you come down to the office in my apartment?"

I said, "Yes," a bit apprehensive, not knowing what to expect. I had never been asked to come to his office before.

As I entered the room, he asked me to sit down. He began by saying, "Well, I guess you know we have had some problems in the hotel recently. Money was stolen and we think we know who did it. But we can't prove it. As a result, we have fired one of the desk clerks. We now find ourselves in a situation where we need another desk clerk. We have observed the way you work. You are conscientious and seem to be honest. Given the situation, we were wondering if you would do us a favor. If we covered your board (food expenses), and paid you $100 more a month, would you be willing to help us out by taking the responsibility of being a desk clerk?"

I thought for a moment and said, "No thank you."

Not really. I actually sat there, amazed, and said, "Yes, I'd be glad to."

Oh, the unexpected, astounding ways of God. Who in the world could have thought up all that occurred?

1) My non-Christian roommate happens to find a flier about jobs in OC (Ocean City, NJ) in a university office, and tells me about it.

2) The Dean of Students calls me on the morning of the interviews, causing me to miss the interviews.

3) The **crazy** thought to write Mr. Snyder and ask for a job pops into my mind one afternoon.

4) I run into a guy named Dave whom I knew freshman year, start talking with him for the first time in over one-and a- half years, find out that he was hired for the job I had requested, and then never see him again.

5) Mr. Snyder receives the letter from his alumni friend raving about another student, and asking for the favor of giving him a job the day before my letter arrives.

6) Mr. Snyder receives and opens Dave's letter refusing the job, and then read my letter.

7) Mr. Snyder wrongly assumes that I am the student his friend raved about, and immediately sends me a letter, offering me the job.

8) My final exam schedule in May enables me to drive to Ocean City and meet Mr. Snyder during one of the weekends when he is there.

9) The decision by Mr. Snyder to give me the job after that awkward moment of silence, even though he realizes I am not the person to whom he intended to give it.

10) The pay, tips and hours being too little to save what I need while also preventing me from getting a second job.

11) God using a robbery to open the door for me to be a desk clerk, and save the money I needed.

Do you call that all-knowing and all-powerful or **what**?

Chapter 9

THREE REASONS FOR GOD'S "BETTER IDEA"

———————∞———————

A s you know, while in college during the summer months, I went to the Jersey shore every weekend I could get away. This practice actually began after my sophomore year in high school. In a way, there was nothing inherently wrong with the desire to get away and have a good time with my friends. Unfortunately, the attitudes and desires associated with meeting and hanging out with different girls every week weren't very good.

After I became committed to following Jesus, I knew I wanted to marry a woman who would similarly be 100 percent committed to fulfilling God's plans for her life. To marry someone less committed than 100 percent could only lead to difficulty in my own seeking and following the Lord. Though this change in perspective had occurred, some of my other patterns of behavior, sadly, hadn't.

As the summer project in Ocean City began, I hate to say it, but I was a "hawk"! Every girl who moved and was part of the project was a "possibility" in terms of meeting, having fun together, and having a potential relationship. During the first week of the project, I surveyed the prospects. At the hotel where I worked, I was able to help a couple Kentucky students on the project get jobs at the hotel. Through them, I met Debbie. Like me, Debbie had just finished her junior year in college. She was pretty with long dark hair, a sweet Southern accent, beautiful blue eyes, and she was athletic, a member of the University of Kentucky tennis team.

As soon as I met her, I said to myself, "Okay, let's see what can happen here."

Over the next two weeks, I went out of my way to talk to her at meetings. One night I asked her if she wanted to get some ice cream on the boardwalk. That night, I also asked if she was going to be on the beach on Saturday. Naturally, I showed up where and when she was going to be on the beach.

Within a short time, it became pretty obvious to Debbie that I was "in pursuit". Perceptive gal! Unfortunately, my efforts did not result in my desired outcome. As we were talking one day, out of the blue she changed the subject, and told me in a sweet yet not-so-sweet way that if I was seeking a relationship with her, that was not going to happen. She also asked me not to invite her to do things if we would be alone.

Wow! Did I ever get **hit** – not physically, of course.

But this did set me back a bit. As I began to reflect on what happened, I realized that though I was only interested in committed Christian girls, I was basically operating like I had since I was in high school. I was just out for the fun, to meet girls, etc. How selfish could I be? I felt ashamed, foolish, and decided "no more of this."

I made a vow to God that I would not seek or have a relationship with any girl on the project that summer. Well, at least I was not going to seek to have a relationship with any girl. They were all going to be my "Christian sisters" and nothing more. In my vow, I added something like, "God, only if You do something extraordinary, something unbelievable, will I even consider a relationship with a girl. I have had it with this stupid, ungodly way of thinking about girls."

Thus, my mind was changed. In a way, having your Aunt Renee at my side made it easier to consider every other girl as being a "sister in the Lord."

Then, one night, something unexpected occurred.

After the outreach meeting on Saturday night, I was sitting on the floor of the room where a lot of the students on the project would hang out after the meetings. My guess is that there were probably thirty of us there that night. One by one, some people I knew left, and I found myself talking to someone whom I had never really known before. Her name was Charlotte – Char — from upstate western New York State. As we talked, I asked about her home and some other questions that I cannot remember.

But there were two other questions that I can recall. I asked her if she had ever been to the beach before. She responded yes, that her family had taken a trip one summer to Boston, and then went to the beach. At that, with complete innocence, I promise, I asked the classic pick-up question: "Have you ever seen the full moon rise over the ocean?" But, it *wasn't* a pick-up line!

She responded, "No."

I said, "It's a beautiful clear night, and soon the moon is going to rise. Do you want to go to the beach and see it?"

Innocently she said, "Okay."

As we got to the beach, the moon had not come up yet. We continued to talk, wrote JESUS in big letters in the sand, and then watched an incredibly beautiful **huge** moon come over the horizon. It reminded me of the night when I had sat on the beach alone, contemplating whether God was real.

I asked her, "Do you want to go see where I accepted Christ last year? It's about a mile down the beach." She agreed.

Down the beach we walked and talked. At the North Street beach, we sat down and I told her my story of how I came to know Christ. She followed by telling me her story.

Before we knew it, it had gotten very late, and I walked her to her apartment. My thoughts never went beyond simply getting to know someone on the project. But as I got back to my "shack" (that's what we called the little buildings out behind the hotel where the workers lived), I thought, *Hmmm God, that was a pretty good and unexpected night. Char's a pretty nice 'sister'. But* **You** *are going to have to do a lot more than cause a nice night with a sister to get me to think any more of it. I am committed to my vow to view all these girls as sisters.*

Little did I know what God had planned. (Though you may have some idea)

As the days went by, I kept running into Char/Grandmom after that night. I **was not** intentionally looking for her. But it seemed that we would casually see each other, and end up talking for a few minutes. She was really easy to talk to, and as a result, the conversations got longer and longer. My guess is that it was about a month later, when I sensed that God might want me to be more intentional about spending time together.

Without a doubt, meeting your Grandmom (Char) was one of the unique things God had planned for that summer. Unfortunately, ha, ha, you will have to wait till another chapter to hear the amazing "God stories" of how our relationship evolved.

I mentioned three reasons that were a part of God's *Better Idea*, and meeting your Grandmom was just one of them.

Midway through the summer, the week for the annual Bystrom family vacation in Ocean City arrived. This summer was a bit different from all the other years of vacation, since for the first time, Aunt Renee and I were already down at the shore. Since we had to work, FarFar and Nana would let us know when they would be at the beach and/or on the boardwalk, so we could meet them when our work schedules allowed it.

One night during that vacation week, Nana and I found ourselves walking and talking on the boardwalk alone. I can remember walking the length of the boards several times as we talked and talked about a relationship with Jesus. It was Nana who had always gone to church, and who had sung to me that song about Jesus so many times. Nana definitely had a heart for God. However, how much she really understood about Jesus being her personal Savior was very fuzzy. And she had no knowledge about how to be filled with the Holy Spirit or walk in His power. As we talked, I saw her heart and desire to be responsive to God. We stopped walking, sat down on a bench on the boardwalk, and prayed for God to confirm things in her heart about Christ being her Savior, and to ask that He would be guiding her in her life.

As I returned to my "shack" that night, I knew it had been a special night.

Exactly what happened that night spiritually in Nana's life, I will not know till heaven. What I do know is that after that night, your Nana's life and relationship with Jesus was never the same. Something *clicked* spiritually in her life. Her understanding of salvation and walking with Jesus took a significant turn in the right direction.

God knew Nana's heart, and I am sure that He would have worked in her life in some other way at some other time if that walk on the boardwalk had not occurred. But seeing what He did that night in Ocean City added one more reason why God had a better idea for my summer than I ever had. **He** is **so good!**

The third reason why God had me go to Ocean City that summer was related to Aunt Renee. The moment my parents said she could go to the beach with me, I knew God wanted me to officially participate in the Summer Beach Project that Cru had. From the first night Renee and I were down there, she participated in all the project meetings. She loved getting to know the college students who were so committed to Christ, hearing all the teaching from the Scriptures, having a personal time with God every day, and as a result, she grew stronger in her faith.

After a summer away from her "friends", she was able to return home and not hang out with the same crowd again. God also provided her with a high school Bible study through an organization called HI-BA, through which she got to know a few other Christian high school students, and continued to be encouraged to grow in her relationship with God.

So, what do you think? I thought that I had the **greatest idea ever**. I could not have been more excited about hitchhiking across the country, but who would you say truly had the **greatest** and **best idea ever**? Me or **God**? (Please tell me you said God!)

That summer I got to see:

1- Nana's life change forever,
2- Aunt Renee's life change forever, and
3- I got to meet my Honey, whom I later married because I was a hitchhiker (that story will come later).

Oh, and those three outcomes don't even recognize what I learned about God's amazing faithfulness and unique ways in providing my first job as a bell boy and my second job as a desk clerk in the hotel.

If I had not believed and recognized that God was smarter than I was, had I not been willing to abandon my own **greatest idea ever** and surrender to His plan which enabled me to meet your Grandmom, most of you who are alive as a part of this family wouldn't exist. God truly did have **the Greatest Idea Ever**.

Chapter 10

The Only Person I Know Who Got Married Because He was a Hitchhiker

———————⊰⊱———————

T his title may surprise you since I met your Grandmom because
I **didn't hitchhike** across the country. However, God works
His will out in our lives, sometimes in surprising ways. Wait till
you hear this one.

The middle of August arrived, and some of the students on
the Cru Summer Project began leaving to go home to get ready to
return to college. Amongst them was your Grandmom. As I drove
her to the Philadelphia airport, I wondered if I would ever see her
again. We had had a great time together after that initial night. It
seemed that God worked in unusual ways so that our schedules
connected, we were able to spend time together, and our friend-
ship/relationship grew. But, the University of Buffalo was a six-
hour drive from my university. To continue the relationship would
require a pretty big commitment. There were no cell phones, no
personal computers back then! We were good friends, but I just
didn't know about continuing the relationship. Thus, as I walked
away from her at the airport, the next time we would meet was,

from my perspective, "totally up in the air." (Sorry, I know this was a **really bad** play on words, but I just couldn't resist it.)

On the Monday morning after her departure, as I awoke, the immediate thought on my mind was, "You have got to get off this little island. You have been boxed in here all summer." Still half asleep, I didn't know what to do with this thought at 6:30am. Thus, I just got up and got ready for work.

As I sat there eating breakfast, the urge/desire to "Get off this little island" reemerged. I shrugged it off again, thinking, *What else do you do with a silly thought like this?*

After work, I ate lunch and went over to the annex of the Lincoln Hotel, where I knew project students would be. To my surprise, a guy named Wes was there. Wes was one of the guys on the project the previous year who had shared with me the Good News about Jesus.

Immediately, I walked up to him and asked, "Wes, what are you doing here?"

He responded, "I had some time off of work, so I thought I'd 'road trip' to a few places. I had a great time here last summer, so I came to see how things were going this year."

I told him my summer had been fantastic, and asked him how long he would be staying.

"I'm leaving for a Christian camp in New York tomorrow" he said.

Ding, Ding, Ding, Ding! Immediately, some bells went off in my mind. *Wes is going to a Christian camp in New York tomorrow. This is my chance to "Get off this little island."* I asked him, "Hey, if I was able to arrange it, could I ride with you to the camp, and then hitchhike back?"

"Sure" he said. "It would be great to have someone to talk to in the car."

Within seconds, I was out the door and back to the hotel. In God's sovereignty and unique plan, the previous week I had worked a day shift for one of the other desk clerks. Thus, he owed me a day of work.

Walking up to him I said, "Hey Tom, I worked a day for you last week, is there any chance you could work for me on Wednesday?"

He said, "Yeah, I can do that. I owe you one. No problem."

I responded, "Great, I need to check out something else, but I will get back to you if it is a go."

Next I was off to find my Bible study leader, a senior from the University of Kentucky. When I found him, I said, "Roy, I have hardly been off the island the entire summer. I have a chance to go to a Christian camp for a day in New York. Is it okay if I just get away for a day or two?"

He said, "That should be fun, go for it."

With that I said, "God, this is great! The way You worked things with Tom and everything. Thanks."

At noon on Tuesday, I finished my shift at the front desk, grabbed some food, my backpack, sleeping bag (I always had my backpack and sleeping bag with me, just in case an opportunity to do something arose), and ran across the street. Wes was waiting. I jumped in the car and off we went. I was so excited to get off the island, to see what God might have in store for a day that would be a little different.

Suddenly I said, "Wes, we just missed our turn."

"No, we didn't," he responded.

"Yes, we did," I said. "The way to New York is up the Garden State Parkway."

"Oh, we're not going up by New York City," he said. "We're going out near Salamanca."

"Salamanca!" "Where's that?"

"About sixty miles south of Buffalo," Wes responded.

"Sixty miles south of Buffalo?!" I think I must have been in a state of mild shock. "I didn't know we were going there!"

Being from South Jersey, if someone talked about a Christian camp in New York, I envisioned a camp in the Catskill Mountains just north of New York City, or possibly the Adirondacks, a mountain range a little further north. I was thinking I would have to hitchhike 100 to 175 miles back to Ocean City on Wednesday. But hitchhiking 400 miles in a day from Western New York was a lot different than what I had in mind. A **lot** different!

Exasperated, I said, "Wes, you need to pull over to the side of the road, I have to pray about this. I had no idea we were going that far." As Wes pulled over and stopped, I began to pray, "God, I don't know what is going on here. I don't want to do this if it isn't okay with You. Lord, please trouble my spirit right now if You don't want me to go." I waited and kind of looked within my mind and spirit to see if I became troubled. As I waited for forty-five quiet seconds, no emotion seemed to stir within me. I then said, "God, if it is okay with You for me to go, just let me sense a peace about it." Again I waited. Everything seemed perfectly fine, no anxiety, just rest within, so I said, "Okay, Wes, **let's go!**"

For me, venturing into the unanticipated was fun and exciting. We went across New Jersey, into Pennsylvania, and then across Pennsylvania on Interstate 80. As we rode, I asked Wes if he had a map. A question had come to my mind: I wondered where Avoca, NY was. I knew Char, your Grandmom, lived in Avoca, but I had no idea where in the state it was. As I looked at the map, it appeared that Avoca was right off Rt. 17. To my surprise, the camp was just off of Rt. 17, about ninety miles west of Avoca.

Hmmm, that's interesting, I thought.

We continued to travel along Interstate 80, until we headed directly north toward the camp. We arrived at about 10pm, just in time to join a Bible study, then about 11:30pm we hit the bunks in one of the cabins.

It was 7:30am when I rolled up my sleeping bag. I decided that I would head back to Ocean City by going west on Rt. 17 past Avoca, and then take Rt. 15 south till I hit Route I-80 again. By 8:15 am, I was on the side of the road on Rt. 17.

As I stood there thinking, I said, "God, if I can make it to Char's before noon, maybe I can give her a call and see her, but if I can't make it there by noon, then I will just continue on the trip since I need to get back to OC tonight." Within a minute of ending the prayer, I got my first ride east. Each time I got dropped off, I didn't have to wait long before someone else picked me up. By 11:30, a guy dropped me off and said, "Avoca is a few miles down the road."

I looked through my wallet to see if I could find the home phone number that Char had given me. There it was! I called, and the phone rang a number of times. I was about to hang up when I heard a, "Hello." It was Char! To say the least, she was a little surprised to hear my voice, and even more surprised to hear that I was about ten miles down the road. I asked her if we could meet, and she said that she would see what she could do. About a half hour later, I was in her car on the way to the farm. I met her dad, ate lunch (score) and then went to the VA hospital where her mom worked, to meet her. At 1:30pm, Char dropped me off on Rt. 17 to again continue my trip.

Unfortunately, after Grandmom dropped me off, the next seven hours were the worst hours of hitchhiking I ever had. The hot August sun beat down on me. I had nothing more to eat or drink. Hour after hour, I stood on the side of the road. A person here, a truck there, would stop, but no one could take me a significant distance.

It was 8:30 that night, I was exhausted and the sun was beginning to set. I had only covered 100 miles since Char dropped me off. 200 miles still remained to get to OC. A truck driver had dropped me off at an exit on I-80 where not even a gas station existed. *What is going on?*, I thought. At 8:40pm I finally said, "God, I just don't know what is happening. I prayed to You about this trip. You know that I have to be at work tomorrow at 7am, and here I am, stuck in the middle of nowhere. No one is picking me up, and I still have 200 miles to go. I just can't stand here any longer. I'm too tired. Lord, I will stand here for another ten minutes, and then if no one picks me up, I will have to go to the side of the road, roll out my sleeping bag and go to sleep. When You know someone is coming that will pick me up, You will just have to wake me up, but I can't stand here any longer."

I looked at my watch to catch the time and waited. Minute after minute went by, and still no one picked me up. Nine minutes passed, then nine minutes fifty seconds. I began to count down the last ten seconds, ten, nine, eight, seven and then **bum, bum, bum, bum, bum**. A large semi-truck was slamming on its brakes, and pulling to the side of the road.

I yelled out, "God, You are so **cool,**" and began running to the truck. As I opened the door, I saw a huge, 260-pound shirtless man, his arm stretched out and his hand behind the curtain into the back compartment. I hesitated and thought, *Do I want to get in here?* But then I thought, *Oh this has to be of God*, and jumped in the cab. The trucker asked me some questions, said that he had been driving all day, and wanted someone he could talk to. He also said that he had a piece (gun) in the back, since he never knew who he might pick up. But he was a friendly guy. He drove me all the way across the rest of Pennsylvania, all the way across New Jersey to the Garden State Parkway.

It was 1am when I got out of the truck. I continued to stick out my thumb, and got three quick rides, but each ride was just a couple miles long, as drivers were on their way home. At 1:30am, feeling that I was getting nowhere fast, and now completely exhausted, I went to the side of the road, rolled out my sleeping bag, and said, "God, this has been quite a day. You know what time I have to be there for work tomorrow morning, so please wake me up in time to get there. Thanks."

I closed my eyes.

Suddenly, **honnnnnnk! honnnnnk**! Someone in a car above me was leaning on his horn. He must have been cut off by another person at the intersection, but the response was enough to wake me up. The night had gone by in what seemed like a second. I rolled up my sleeping bag, went to the road's edge, and stuck out my thumb. The second car picked me up and dropped me off at the Ocean City exit. I walked beyond the toll booth, stuck out my thumb, and the first car picked me up. He dropped me off right in front of the hotel.

What time was it? If you don't know from hearing this story before, **make a guess.** What time do you think it was when I arrived at the hotel?

I'll tell you in a little bit. *Ha, Ha.*

There are so many specific details about this trip that just make me shake my head. It is astounding that we can have a God who is so personal. He works through our personalities and tendencies to work out His perfect will. He knows the details of every situation. Think about this:

1) He caused a non-Christian co-worker (Tom) to ask me to work a day for him the week before this trip.
2) He woke me up that Monday morning with a rather ridiculous thought in my mind: *Get off this little island.*
3) He had Wes travel into town and caused me to run into him that Monday afternoon.
4) He enabled Tom to work for me on Wednesday.
5) He caused my Bible study leader to give me permission to leave for the trip (I can assure you, this would never happen with the present day Cru summer mission policies).
6) He caused Wes to go to a Christian camp in Western New York, right off of Rt. 17.
7) God did not trouble my heart and emotions when I prayed for His guidance, and He allowed a calmness to continue as I asked for peace.

8) He got me near Char's home by 11:30am with three quick rides.

9) He got me a free lunch (yeah), and I got to meet Char's mom and dad (I will never know if my meeting Char's dad on that day contributed to his unexpected and undesired response to a question we asked him months later — that's another story).

10) He allowed me to be stuck in a desolate spot on Interstate 80 with the sun going down, and then during my ten-second countdown in His omniscient timing, God caused a truck to pull over and pick me up.

11) He had the truck driver take me 150 miles and drop me off at the Garden State Parkway.

12) He arranged it so one driver cut off another person early in the morning, so that I woke up.

13) AND, he got me dropped off at the hotel at? **What time did you guess?** It was 6:55am.

I ran to my shack, washed up, shaved as quickly as I could, and ran into work.

There are many lessons that can be learned from this adventure, but for me, the **most significant** part of this story is that as I reflected on the trip afterwards, I concluded that if God went to that much trouble to get me to see Char, your future Grandmom, again, maybe **He** wanted me to pursue the relationship. And with that in mind, I did.

To this day I am the only person I know who got married because he was a hitchhiker.

Chapter 11

A Surprise? Not Really

———————⊶✕⊷———————

I t was my senior year at college. I had been back at school two weekends. Since the memorable hitchhiking trip in August, Char and I had been writing each other once or twice a week. I was amazed at her thoughtful reflections as she wrote about various circumstances, blending her comments with humor, creativity, and trust in God.

As was my norm in decision making in those days, usually last minute, I decided to go up to see her late on Thursday night. Since I really didn't know when I would see her, and since I was one who liked to surprise people, I didn't give her even the slightest hint that I might be coming. I decided not to let her know I was on my way until I was relatively close to the University of Buffalo. I could get to Buffalo without a problem. But getting to her dorm or a meeting place would best be accomplished after talking to her and gaining some final directions.

About an hour outside of Buffalo, I decided to pull off the road, find a phone booth and give her a call. (Cell phones didn't exist back then. Thus the telephone company stationed phone booths at gas stations, shopping malls, and other locations where people might need to call someone.)

Little did I know what God was up to **before** I called. I will let Grandmom share what occurred in her life that afternoon.

Grandmom...

It started out as a pretty normal Friday of classes and no big plans for the weekend. Then, late afternoon, something changed. There was no audible voice, nothing that seemed totally shocking at the moment, but I was struck by a really clear sense that I needed to clean up my dorm room because Ron was coming for a visit. He hadn't called or hinted. Not in the slightest. It didn't even seem odd to me at the time. Nothing could have been more clear or normal...to me.

Just as I was about to pull the mop out in the final sweep (tile floor and no carpeting), my friends came down the hall so we could head off to the dining hall for dinner.

"What's going on? Why are you the mopping the floor?" they asked. They were obviously curious. It's not often that a dorm room floor gets a good mopping! When I told them Ron was coming to visit, they were excited with me! "When did he call?"

As soon as I told them my story and how it seemed God had given me a "heads up," they said they would be back in a minute and they headed back down the hall. Later I understood why...two of the gals had been walking in relationship with Jesus for years and were seriously concerned that I was more likely to be operating on my hopes rather than truly hearing something from God. So they gathered to pray that the disappointment wouldn't negatively affect my comparably new relationship with Jesus. Great friends with all the best intentions and concerned hearts, but God was about to expand our understanding of just how personal He can show Himself in our everyday lives!

Seems I had some last-minute finishing touches yet to do after the floor dried, so my friends left a few minutes ahead of me to get a place in line at the dining hall. Just as I was about to close and lock my door, the phone rang. It was Ron! Seriously! He was just one hour away (at least a six-hour trip in total)!

It still makes me smile through and through to remember the looks on the faces of my friends when I told them! God was doing some incredible things early on in our relationship to demonstrate how great He was and, I think, to confirm that He was the one who had bought us together for whatever His purposes might be at this point and for our future! In the process, our "small God" was getting bigger!

Chapter 12

"What Have I Done?"
"Count to Ten"

———————⟡———————

D eep within my heart and spirit, I was wrestling and wrestling. Day and night, the question was there: *Should I, or shouldn't I ask Char to marry me?* As I prayed and looked back over the last nine months, it was obvious that God had brought us together, that He was behind the events of our relationship, and that a love for each other had grown. We had:

1) Begun our relationship with God orchestrating things from the very first night we met
2) Continued our relationship because of a crazy hitchhiking experience and circumstances that only God could have imagined and arranged
3) Written two or more times a week over a seven-month period of time
4) Met at her home many times, which interestingly was halfway between my school and the University of Buffalo. This saved time, travel, enabled me to get to know her family, and the surroundings in which she grew up better

5) A great time of fun sharing and talking when she came down for the annual fraternity Christmas party

6) By phone, letters, or just in talking when we were together, shared the deepest, most challenging, and difficult parts of our lives with each other

7) Let our individual desire to serve the Lord in full-time vocational ministry, if God called, be known to each other

8) Talked about all our other hopes and dreams related to having children, financial ambitions or lack thereof, and trusting and following God in complete surrender.

Every area we discussed seemed to line up. We were in basic agreement in our hearts, our hopes, our fears, and in the future that God might have for us. Our love for and attraction to each other had also grown and deepened week by week, month by month. But the question remained: *Should I ask Char to marry me? Does God want us to take that next* **huge, huge, huge,** *life-altering, 'for the rest of our lives' commitment?* "Oh God, what do You want us to do, me to do?" This was my constant plea for weeks.

It was a cold night in March. Char and I were meeting that weekend at her home. Snow was on the ground, and we asked her folks if we could go up to the family cabin for a few hours that Saturday night, to which they said yes.

The cabin was a two-story building built on the foundation of the old Towner homestead. Her grandfather grew up in the original house from which they used to trade with the native Indians in that region. Downstairs was one large room. In it there was a potbelly stove, a bathroom, a chest of drawers, and two twin beds. Upstairs was a large room with a beautiful stone fireplace, a kitchen area with a stove, sink, and a raised counter with stools around it. A sofa and a couple soft chairs were set in front of the fireplace area. As the fire blazed, it truly was a romantic setting to pop the question, if that was what I was going to do.

As we sat there, multiple conversations were simultaneously going on in my mind. I was having that ongoing discussion with God. "Should I, or shouldn't I? Should I, or shouldn't I? Should I, or shouldn't I?"

Flitting in and out of my mind, in between my words in conversation with Char, were memories of the last nine months, what had happened, the things we had talked about, the good and the hard times, what they all meant and/or didn't mean for the future. As I continued to pray, "Oh God, what should I do?" I became confident that He was the one who had brought us together, that He was the one who had been leading us through the previous nine months, and that He was doing it for a purpose. The purpose was that we should be together, serving Him together for the rest of our lives.

With that thought in my mind, I conjured up every ounce of courage within me and finally said something like, "Char, I have something to ask you. I believe that God has led us in our relationship since last summer and that He wants us to have a relationship together in the future. I love you and want to ask you, Char, will you marry me?" (Specifically what I said, I honestly cannot remember, but I am sure it was something like that.)

Char looked up at me, smiled, put her head on my shoulder and then snuggled a bit. But she said nothing. In silence I waited, and waited. But still, nothing. Inside, I began to squirm. *What is she thinking? What is she really saying or not saying?*

Finally, I couldn't take it any longer! (In actuality, it was probably fifteen seconds of silence. But it seemed like "forever" in the moment). I said, "Char, are you going to say anything? Do you want to marry me?"

At that she looked up and said, "Of course! Didn't you know that by how I responded?"

(Inside I said, "Ahhh, No. A non-verbal response doesn't tell me what you are thinking.") I followed with my own non-verbal response, gave her a hug, and said, "I love you."

This time she responded with, "I love you, too," and a kiss.

We decided that night that it wasn't the right time to share our intentions and desires with her parents. We simply went back to their house and went to our separate rooms to sleep.

Then it happened…

The next morning, Sunday, I woke up. Immediately my mind went to thinking about Char. But as I did, emotionally there was **nothing**.

Immediately I thought, *Oh man. What is going on? Did I make a mistake? Did I misread God's will?* I tried to convince myself that the absence of any emotion was just a temporary circumstance. *Wait for ten or fifteen minutes and everything will be fine*, I thought.

Unfortunately, it wasn't fine after ten minutes. It wasn't fine after fifteen minutes. It wasn't fine after one, two, or three hours! I didn't know what to do. As I went upstairs to the kitchen, I tried to hide what was going on inside and act normal. But, I intentionally kept my distance from Char as we had breakfast with her parents and brother. Then I disappeared down the stairs to the bathroom, took a shower as long as I possibly could, got dressed, packed some things, and disappeared in my room to have a personal time with the Lord. The longer I could avoid seeing Char, the better.

Just after lunch, Dan Earl and his girlfriend (future wife) Jenny, arrived. They were good friends from the University of Buffalo. We went for a long walk down the road and up towards the cabin. I tried to position myself on the other side of the foursome from Char so that I wouldn't feel obligated to hold her hand. She sensed something was wrong, but we weren't able to talk since Dan and Jenny were there. They were going to give her a ride back to the University of Buffalo and soon I would be on my way south towards Pennsylvania. For me, the sooner the better!

After we returned from the walk, it was time to leave. As quick as I could, I grabbed my bags. I gave Grandmom a weak hug, a pitiful, quick kiss, jumped in the car, and took off. I couldn't stand being in her presence, feeling like such a fool and hypocrite.

As I drove away, the more I thought about the situation, the worse I felt. **What have I done?** *Did I deceive myself and Char into thinking I was in love? Have I totally misread the leading of the Lord? Should I break off the engagement right away, or wait? What should I do?* One thing I did know, I had created a mess. In the car, I became so emotionally upset and began crying so hard, I had to pull over to the side of the road. In one sense, I couldn't believe I was crying. Except for one situation when I was a lot younger, I couldn't remember ever crying. *Guys didn't cry*, or so I was told. But that day in the car, I couldn't help myself.

It seemed that every time I calmed down a bit and began to drive, I would begin crying and had to pull to the side of the road. Instead of three hours, it took me about four-and-a-half hours to get back to school. I immediately went to my room and wrote Char a letter. In it, I said that something huge was going on in my life. That I couldn't be honest with myself and say that I loved her. I apologized, said I had to sort things out with God, and asked her not to call or be in touch in any way until I knew what the Lord wanted. I again apologized, and just signed it, Ron.

Char returned to her university, knowing that something was up, but not sure what. So she let all her friends know I had pro-posed to her. Immediately her girlfriends went into high planning mode, talking about when and how they could have a shower for her. There was a buzz of excitement within the Cru movement on campus.

But then she received my letter. Naturally, she was shocked to see what I wrote. She immediately wanted to call, but also wanted to honor my request to not call or be in touch in any way. Thus, she simply told her closest friends and all of them began to pray.

Back at school, I hardly slept Sunday night. I tossed and turned all night, trying to make sense out of things. It seemed that all I could do was cry and remain confused. On Monday morning, I went to my 9am Greek class. About halfway through the class, the professor asked me a question. I realized that I had not heard the question, or anything else he said during the entire class. I apologized and said, "I am sorry, I think I should leave class."

He said, "That would be fine. If there is anything that I can do, let me know."

I said, "Thanks, I will," and walked out the door.

I went to the frat house and tried to avoid having anyone see me. Once in my room, all I could do was cry over what I had done. Our Christian fellowship group met every night at 5pm to pray. I went and shared with everyone what was going on and asked them to pray for wisdom for me. To me, one of two things was happening. Either I had misread the Lord's leading, which meant that I needed to break up with Char, call off the engagement and the relationship, or, I was in the midst of a battle with my flesh and Satan. If this was the case, the exact opposite response was needed. I needed to ignore the immediate absence of feelings, trust that God had been faithfully leading me, and continue to walk by faith. Which way I should go? I didn't have a clue.

I didn't go to any classes on Tuesday. I cried, prayed, and continued to try to figure things out. All with no success. Around dinner time, I called the home of the Dean of Students, said I was facing a serious problem, and asked if I could come to his home and seek counsel from him and his wife. That night after they put the kids to bed, I drove over to share with them what was happening. They were very kind, but had never heard of anyone experiencing what I was going through. They recommended that I not get married if this was the way I felt.

Wednesday was another horrible day. Once again, I didn't go to any classes. In fact, I didn't go to any classes the rest of the week. I couldn't get this off my mind, nor could I think of anything else. On Thursday, I became kind of numb. Emotionally, I dried up and couldn't cry anymore. I simply groaned inside as I wrestled with what I should do. But no further insight was given.

On Friday night, at the 5 o'clock prayer meeting, I pulled two of my most trusted friends aside, and asked them to fast and pray with me over the weekend. On Monday night, we would gather together, and each of us would share what he or she felt the Lord was indicating: 1) to break off the relationship because I had misread the Lord's leading, or, 2) recognize it as a weakness in the flesh/spiritual battle, tell Char that all was good, and that I'd like to move ahead in faith. They agreed to join me.

Through the weekend and Monday, I fasted and continually thought and prayed. Finally about 4pm on Monday, I sensed a breakthrough had been made. It seemed to me that I was undergoing spiritual battle. A battle was raging to take me away from God's best for my life. Though this thought seemed to be settling within me, I was thankful that I would be getting together with my two friends later that night.

As we got together, I told them that I felt that I had a breakthrough in terms of what was going on, but that I needed to hear from them before I said what it was. Silence. Each friend wondered who should speak first. Finally, one of them said she was persuaded to think that it was spiritual battle, and that I should move ahead in my relationship with Char. The second person said he agreed, and he also thought it was spiritual battle. I told them this was exactly what I had sensed. We hugged each other, spent some time in prayer giving thanks, yet continued to acknowledge that all we wanted was what God wanted.

As I left the Chapel auditorium where we prayed, it felt as if a huge weight had been lifted from me. I immediately went to the frat house, and I couldn't wait to call Char.

But, on her end, a lot had also been taking place.

Grandmom…

Let's go back to that walk up the hill to the cabin the day after the proposal. What a strange walk that was! The very person who had declared his love and asked me to spend the rest of my life with him was now out of step with me, and didn't even want to hold my hand. In fact, it seemed intentional on his part **not** to walk close to me at all. When I asked if there was anything wrong, there wasn't much of a response. Actually, I think he might have said something like, "Ahh, we can talk about it later."

Once I was back on campus, though, the excitement of the proposal overrode the strangeness of that Sunday walk to the cabin, and soon my closest friends joined in the excitement. A "surprise" shower was being planned within days! Then, the letter came in my mailbox…

I was shocked and devastated…How could his love turn **so** cold **so** quickly after the proposal that he took **so** seriously? How could I have been **so** sure that he was the one God had for me? How would I ever be able to be sure about anything in the future, especially about the one God had for me to share the rest of my life with as my husband? There were more questions than answers that flooded my mind and heart.

My dear friend, Lynda, shared many a tear and hours of prayer and searching with me behind the closed door of my room. We were together on our knees, as I struggled to understand and, at first, tried to figure out how it made sense. It didn't. It was a struggle to see God's goodness, His kindness in the midst of all the emotional hurt. So, together we talked to God, spilling out all the hurt, all the disappointment. "Why would You let this happen, God?"

God doesn't give us any guarantees that things in life will make sense, at least not while we are still on this earth. He **does** show us and tell us over and over again in the Scriptures that He loves us, that He is with us. God was even showing His love to me by leading us to verses like Matthew 11:28-30:

> "Come to Me, all who are weary and heavy laden, and I will give you rest. Take My yoke upon you, and learn from Me, for I am gentle and humble in heart and YOU SHALL FIND REST FOR YOUR SOULS. For My yoke is easy, and My burden is light."

I was weary. My heart was aching and heavy with hurt and confusion. He was gentle and I needed a big dose of His kind of gentleness and His rest. I needed to learn how to come to Him and give Him this relationship, no matter what it would mean for the future. God's best for me was God's best, not what I thought God's best would, could, or should be. Does that make sense? Nothing escapes His attention. He sees all things. And He is putting the pieces of our lives together in a way that will create something beautiful... like the pieces of a puzzle. Some of those pieces, all by themselves, don't always look like they fit. You know. You have put together lots and lots of puzzles. Some of those pieces are really hard to see how they fit into the big picture. But they do! It is like that with many things in our lives — they just don't seem to fit! At least not the way we think they should. Some of the most precious times of life come with tears of searching and surrender, and sharing those times in prayer and tears with a friend. I will be forever grateful to my friend, Lynda, for being there with me in such a difficult time and helping me find my peace, my rest, my comfort in who God is and the truths of His Word.

As the days ticked away it became more and more difficult **not** to hear anything from Ron...there were no calls, no letters, and of course, back then there were no emails or text messages. Finally, it felt like I couldn't bear another minute of not knowing what was going on in his thinking, in his heart, in his mind. Though I wanted to honor his request to wait to hear first from him, how long was I to wait? I was having a really, really hard time waiting. Finally, I was done with waiting. Oh, how thankful I am that God is so very patient and knows our weak spots.

Now, as strange and made-up as this next part may sound to you, believe me, it felt just as strange to me. Big time strange! But oh, so real, none-the-less. And it really did happen, just like this:

My mind was made up! I went to the phone in my room — the kind with the cord and the handle — and as my hand was positioned inches away to pick up the phone, a voice in my head, clearly and with a sense of authority I couldn't ignore, said, "Before you pick up the phone, count to ten." It was so bizarre that I stopped with my hand ready to pick up the phone, shook my head, and tried again. And again, the voice said, "Count to ten."

"Fine!" I said out loud, with a bit of stubborn confusion, and I started to count: "One, two, three, four, five, six, seven, eight, nine..." As soon as I said "ten," the phone rang. No kidding! Startled, I picked it up, and with a question in my voice, said, "Hello?" I'm not sure **who** I expected to be on the other end at that point, but I figured it was important and I had better listen! And you can probably guess who it was. Right? It was Ron.

How amazing is that? He had called to explain everything, and say he loved me. All was well. I was crying again, but this time it was because God had kept me from making that call, so that I would have the joy of Ron calling me instead, and honoring his request **not** to call him.

What an extraordinary thing God had done with the "count to ten" experience! Clearly He was protecting me from going against Ron's wishes that I **not** initiate, but wait for him to call. And it was a miraculous, extraordinary blessing to know so clearly that I needed to count to ten before I would call, only to have the phone ring and it was Ron calling me! It really did happen just like that!

Exactly! Isn't God amazing? He doesn't often seem to do things in such extraordinary ways, but He **is** God, and He can and does reveal Himself and His care for us in many, many ways — some that may seem more profound than others.

Granddad …

I am thankful and humbled to say that since that Monday night, there has never again been another moment of doubting my love for your Grandmom or that God wanted us together.

Chapter 13

OUR NEXT SURPRISE

———————∝———————

N ow that this spiritual and emotional test had been overcome, you might expect, as we did, that from here on out it would be smooth sailing. Guess what? Not so!

Grandmom (Char) and I knew her dad would have a lot of questions for me about providing for his one and only daughter. In preparation for asking for his blessing to marry, we discussed all the possible questions he might ask. We thought through our schedule over the weeks ahead and determined that the best time to approach her dad, asking for his blessing, would be on the first weekend of our college spring breaks, which amazingly fell on the same week.

Char and I met at her parents' home the first Friday night of spring break. The plan was to:

1) get her dad's/parents' approval,
2) head down to my parents in South Jersey on Sunday and make the fantastic announcement that we would be getting married,
3) go into Philadelphia to Samson Street, the diamond/jewelry district, and buy the rings,

4) go back to my fraternity house on Friday, with Char continuing back to her home for the weekend before she returned to school on Sunday.

Sounds like a plan, huh?

On Saturday night, just as we were finishing dinner, probably after squirming in my seat most of the meal, I said, "Mr. Towner, I was wondering if I could ask you something after dinner in the living room?" He looked at me and made a slight grunt, which I took as a yes. As we got up from the table, Grandmom's dad and I walked into the living room and sat down. Silently, I was praying, "Oh God, please help me now."

I began by saying something like, "As you know, Char and I met last summer, and our relationship and commitment to one another has continued to grow over the last nine months. We have been talking and praying about it a lot, and we would like to ask for your blessing to get married after Char graduates from college this summer." Little did I know the full scope of what was about to happen.

Yes, we anticipated some tough questions, but nothing like what was about to begin.

I didn't just receive a few questions, but for the next forty minutes, Char's dad challenged me with question after question. Actually, every question we thought of in our preparatory brainstorming was asked, and then some. Calmly, I sought to impress him with how much I/we had thought through, how concerned and committed I was to adequately provide for his only daughter, while silently praying with each ensuing question, "God, give me wisdom."

As the forty-minute drilling ended, he said, "Why don't you go into the other room and ask Char to come here. I want to talk to her." I went into the den, where Char and her mom had turned on the TV. I told Char her dad wanted to talk to her. As she passed, I raised my eyebrows as a non-verbal way to say, *I don't know, but I think things went okay.* Slowly, she disappeared into the living room.

Twenty minutes later, Char reappeared and said, "Mom, Dad wants to talk to you."

Quietly, her mom rose and went into the other room. In her absence, Char and I talked about what had taken place. We both felt that we had answered his questions well, demonstrating that we hadn't taken this step lightly. Before we knew it, within a few minutes, Char's mom reappeared at the door. She said, looking at Char, "Your dad would like to speak to both of you." As we walked into the living room, we both fully expected a rather begrudging, "Yes, you have my blessing."

Shock, unbelief, bewilderment, and sadness enveloped us as we heard him say something like, "Well, I've considered your request for my blessing and I will not give it to you. If the two of you really love each other, then that love will last, and after two or three years, maybe I'll change my mind." Then, looking at me, he said, "You can go down to south Jersey and get that job you said was there for you. Char, you can return home and get a nursing job nearby. I have made up my mind, and this ends the discussion." He got up and left the room.

Stunned, Char and I couldn't move. We looked at each other in total disbelief. We looked at her mom and she immediately got up and walked out of the room. What were we to do? Neither of us could speak.

Finally I said, "Let's go for a walk." We got up, put on our coats, still unable to say another word, and walked into the cold night air.

As we walked along the little-used back road that ran past their house, gradually words began to come out. I cannot recall exactly what was said by whom that night. But two outcomes were definitely determined. First, we could not get married without her dad's blessing. Second, we needed to pray about this a ton.

What would this mean for us? Where would it lead us?

As we walked along the road that night, we stopped talking to each other and began talking to God. "Oh God, we really do not know what to do, except come to You. God, please help us know what to do. We really feel that You have brought us together, that You have guided us step by step in our relationship. But now this has happened. God, we know that we can't get married against Char's dad's wishes. Lord, all we can do is to ask You to change his heart, to change his mind. We don't know how, but we simply ask You to do it, continue to lead us. Continue to give us hearts that want to be surrendered to You in every way, to trust You and follow You. In Jesus' name we pray. Amen."

The next day, Sunday afternoon, we said goodbye to her parents and drove to New Jersey to see my family. We decided not to say a word to my family about my proposal to Char. As we continued to pray, we continued to ask God for a change of heart in her dad. But we knew this was no easy task. Char's dad was a farmer, set in his ways. Once he decided something, it was virtually impossible to change his mind. Yet, we prayed, and believed in spite of this reality, God was able.

As a result, one day during the next week, without anyone in my family knowing, we went into Philadelphia to explore the possibilities for engagement and wedding rings. Since Christ was at the center of our relationship, we decided to have the diamond set in the middle of a cross on the engagement ring. The wedding ring would slide under the engagement ring so that the two would be connected. For me, I wanted a simple gold band, similar to the one that I had always seen on my dad's finger. That afternoon, we were excited to find out that what we wanted could be made. Our fingers were sized and the specific instructions for Char's rings were confirmed. Everything was set, except that we told them that we would get back to them on when the rings should be made. That is, after God performed the miracle of changing Char's dad's heart.

Friday afternoon, we arrived at my fraternity house. Before Char left to go home, I asked her not to mention anything about the engagement that night. I asked her to go home and be his little girl on Friday night and Saturday. Then maybe bring up the subject on Sunday before she left for school. My worst fear was that she would walk through the door and almost immediately the issue would erupt, resulting in an undesirable outcome.

Just before 7pm, one of my fraternity brothers yelled down the hall, "Hey Bystrom, you have a call from Char."

Immediately I thought, *Oh no. She walked in the door and the worst thing imaginable happened.* With instantaneous discouragement, I walked to the phone. I said, "Hi Char," and she said, "Ron you won't believe it. I walked through the door and Mom told me that Dad had changed his mind. We can get married this summer."

Excitedly I yelled, "What? I can't believe it!"

We laughed and I think almost cried.

Marriage, here we come!

Chapter 14

DEATH OF A DREAM

F arFar pushed back his chair, leaned over the table and yelled, **"What are you going to do, become a fanatic?"** Shocked, and in every way surprised, I could not believe my ears. Or, what I saw.

My dad, otherwise known to your mom as FarFar, was somewhat the stereotypical Swede: A man who essentially held his emotions within; a man of very few words. Though I can't recall my dad ever saying the words "I love you" as I was growing up, there was never a day when I didn't know that he loved me. He demonstrated his love through his caring ways, and by working a minimum of fifty-five hours a week. Most of that time, he was standing in one spot as he meticulously worked his skill, cutting down carbide pieces with .0001 of an inch accuracy. FarFar was very well known and respected for his skill by others in his trade.

As FarFar was growing up, his family became very poor. His parents traveled on a ship from Sweden to America in 1919. They didn't know a word of English. All they had heard of was the "American Dream". That dream basically was, if you came to America and worked hard, you could provide for your family and become a success. FarFar's dad was a skilled carpenter and for the first ten years that they lived in America, the "American Dream" seemed to be working. After a brief time on Long Island, NY, they settled in south Jersey. FarFar's dad built them a large home, and things were going great. Then the Great Depression of 1929 hit. The first individuals to lose their jobs and the last ones able to obtain work were recent immigrants who knew little English and spoke with strong accents. FarFar's dad was one of them. As a result of being out of work, they couldn't pay the bills on the new large home. Thus, they sold it and FarFar's dad built a second, smaller home. After some time passed, they also lost this home due to the absence of a job. During the stretches of time when work couldn't be found, the family would eat apple butter on bread for all three meals. When FarFar's oldest sister (Aunt Inge) was sixteen, she had to quit school, leave the home, and begin working as a maid for some of the remaining wealthy people in Philadelphia. To say the least, very hard times were experienced by FarFar and his family during the Great Depression.

While FarFar was still in high school, he met a really fun and exciting girl, the one you know as Nana. They dated their junior and senior years in high school. After FarFar graduated from high school in 1939, he got a job at SKF, a factory that made ball bearings. As World War II began, he was able to get a deferment from joining the Army since the product SKF produced was extremely necessary for the Army to function. In 1942, your FarFar and Nana got married. A year later, he was drafted into the Army and ended up going to Germany.

After World War II, FarFar returned home and as was the case for many of the young couples of that day, FarFar and Nana were interested in starting a family. As a result, FarFar never ended up going to college, but rather became a skilled surface grinder in a factory.

I share this with you so you can know a little more about my family's past, but also, because these experiences had a big effect on how FarFar approached life as an adult and parent.

The Monday night after I placed my faith in Christ, as I sat at the dinner table, I had planned to tell my parents the "Fantastic News" of how I came to know Christ after we finished the main meal and were about to eat dessert. But I guess I was squirming in my chair, because halfway through the meal, Nana said to me, "Ron, do you have something to tell us, you're acting a little different tonight." As I heard those words, silently I exclaimed, "YES!"

I began to share with them how in January I had rejected Christianity, how I became very antagonistic towards it and then met students on the beach who for the first time in my life, explained their Christianity in what I considered to be an intelligent way. I told them that every weekend I had been going down to the beach to spend time with them, to read the books that they recommended, and that finally on Saturday night I said something like, "Jesus, I do not know if You are alive right now or if I am like some idiot talking to the air... but if You are alive, if You can hear my voice right now, I want You to reveal Yourself to me, to come into my life, to be my Savior because I definitely need one, and to begin doing all the things You said You would do." I continued on a roll about how excited I was that God could lead me in my life.

That was when my dad pushed back his chair and yelled at me. The words, "What are you going to do, become a fanatic?" had a lot of passion to them. I can only remember my dad yelling at me one other time in my life, when I was twelve or thirteen. I can't recall exactly what I did, but I vaguely remember that I had done something really dumb! Now, at twenty years of age my dad was leaning over the table and yelling at me as loud as he could. What was going on?

Then he did something I will never forget. As I mentioned, during the tough times of the Great Depression, his family ate apple butter on bread for all three meals for stretches at a time. The result of this experience caused food to be viewed as **very precious**. As I was growing up, none of us were allowed to leave or throw away as much as a pea from our plate. That pea, every pea, any food, was too precious to be wasted and thrown away.

But that night, my dad not only yelled at me in anger, he got up from the table halfway through dinner, left the food on his plate, and never came back to eat it. **WOW! Why** was he **so upset**?

I didn't understand it at the moment, but later it made sense. It was because, as I was growing up, my dad lived and worked hard not only to provide for his family, but to see one important dream fulfilled. That was to have his son — his one and only son — grow up, go to college, be a success, and bring honor to the Bystrom name. What I accomplished would be the fulfillment of his life dream, and the dream that his parents had when they came to America from Sweden.

Immediately, FarFar saw my commitment to Christ as a threat to the fulfillment of his parents' and his life dream.

The truly astounding reality related to how FarFar responded was…he was exactly right in his prediction and fears. Two years later, after I graduated from college, my heart's desire was to go into full-time Christian ministry. And the worst thing was, to fulfill the ministry to which I felt led, I would have to "beg people for money."

It truly was a painful death to FarFar's **life dream**.

But why do I share this with you?

I share it because of the battle that this caused within me. I truly loved my dad and I truly wanted him to be proud of me. A part of me wanted to fulfill his life dream, and yet it seemed that I was unable to do this while also fulfilling what I felt God had put on my heart.

To me, the most fantastic possibility someone could have in this life <u>was not</u> to become wealthy, or even to personally know and have a relationship with a President of the United States. Nor would it be to have the President come to me and say, "Ron, I like you and respect you. Would you fulfill this role or job for me?" No, the greatest privilege of one's life would be to know the Creator of the universe, to have Him work in your life, and then to have Him lead and guide you to fulfill His plan and purposes for your life.

What a tremendous life transformation can occur when someone gets to know God, is able to know and experience God's love every day (or almost every day), realizes that he or she is "His workmanship, created in Christ Jesus for good works, which God prepared beforehand,"(Ephesians 2:10) walks in them, and fulfills them. And on top of that, has his eternal destiny changed from eternal separation from God to being fulfilled forever in God's presence.

If I could be involved in helping others know this, to see their lives dramatically changed now and forever, what better activity or purpose could there be than to spend all my time and energy devoted to seeing this occur? Personally, I could think of nothing that was as great, significant, or desirable.

Yet as I contemplated this desire, I recognized it could not be fulfilled without rejecting my dad's life purpose. It is similar to what many Christian students who desire to go into full-time Christian vocational ministry face. They have grown up hearing their parents' expectations, or the expectations of teachers, professors, relatives, etc. With this knowledge, the critical question can emerge, "Who is Lord of your life? Is it your dad, mom, professor, etc., and fulfilling their dreams and hopes for your life, or is it God?" Though I loved my dad and was very committed to always acting in a respectful and honoring way towards him, I realized that Jesus had to be my Lord, my boss, the one guiding me to fulfill His will and purposes for my life. To follow and fulfill the desires of my dad or any other person, would nullify Jesus truly being my Lord.

Having established this conclusion, a second aspect, and for me a more difficult issue arose. The question was: "Is God guiding you into full-time Christian vocation, or is this just what you want to do?" Was entering full-time vocational ministry my will or the Lord's will? This was the question I struggled with for several months.

Your Grandmom and I decided to get married on July 15th. This date was chosen in large measure because Grandmom had to take two more classes during the months of May thru early July to obtain her bachelor of science degree in nursing. I graduated in May with a degree in psychology and went to work for the company where FarFar had been the first hired employee, and where I had worked since I was sixteen.

Our plan was for me to work there before and after our marriage while we sought the Lord in terms of our long-term ministry or other vocations. The lordship testing related to full-time vocational ministry versus another job grew during this time.

The name of the President, CEO, and chief salesman of the company where I worked was Jack. The summer I graduated from college, Jack was fifty-seven years old. Having worked for the company for six years (after school two afternoons a week and Saturday mornings during my junior and senior year in high school; full time every summer except the summer project summer), they had gotten to know me, my work ethic, sense of responsibility, etc. I had worked in every department of the business except for the skilled die making work, which was what FarFar did, and in the front office.

The potential idea and job that emerged in <u>my mind</u> was as follows: I would work for approximately two years in the front office under Jack, get to know the office functions, while also talking to our customers on the phone when appropriate. Then, I would begin to travel with Jack to the customers in the US and Europe that he had established over his thirty-five years in the business. As the years passed and my relationship with those customers strengthened, one by one, Jack would stop traveling, and they would become my customers. Additionally, during this time, I would be expected to acquire new customers. The end result would be that

I would receive the commissions for new purchase contracts from all of Jack's past customers, as well as any new customers I established. The potential income in my estimation could be hundreds of thousands of dollars a year within the next seven years and beyond.

It truly seemed to be a one-in-a-million opportunity. Plus, it would enable me to fulfill every aspect of FarFar's life dream. But my heart's passion was not in making money. I wanted to devote 100 percent of my time towards seeing lives changed, now and forever.

In a similar way, Grandmom wanted to give 100% of her time towards reaching others. In the field of nursing in the 1970's, sharing anything spiritual with a patient was strongly forbidden. On the one hand, Grandmom liked caring for the physical needs of people. However as she was daily with patients, she realized their greatest need was not physical healing, but spiritual healing. Being prohibited from addressing the greater need in any way was very difficult for her emotionally. As a result, her desire to be a nurse diminished as her desire to be in vocational ministry rose.

Through the months of June, July, and August as I worked at the company, we both struggled with what we were going to do. Part of our difficulty was the lack of peace we had when we thought about going to the Cru training. At one point, it was as if God was asking us if we were willing to do *anything* for him: full-time vocational ministry or secular jobs. Anything. We realized how set our hearts were on going the direction of ministry. Few people feel this way, but we did! That was a revelation for us. God was wanting us to surrender to Him, and that surrender meant being willing to work at the company for me and a nursing position for Char.

Recognizing this one night in bed, I said, "Okay, Lord. If You want me to work long term at this company rather than full-time vocational ministry, I am willing. You are LORD, not me!"

About 9am the next morning, Jack walked up to me and said, "Hey Ron, why don't we go to lunch today?"

Immediately I thought, "Wow, I surrendered to God last night, and first thing this morning, Jack is asking me to go to lunch with him." Though I had worked at the company for six years, Jack had never asked me to go to lunch with him.

As we sat down at the restaurant, the normal talk about family, sports, and Jack's airplane began. Midway through the lunch, Jack transitioned and said something like, "I imagine you are wondering why I asked you to lunch. I have been thinking about you and your situation a lot. You know that you can have a future with the company, but I also know that you have been considering full-time ministry and going to some training that is being offered in October. I have a recommendation for you. I would encourage you to take time off, go out to that training, and decide what you want to do with your life."

I was shocked and surprised! After surrendering and being willing to take the job the night before, when Jack asked me to go out for lunch the next morning, my assumption was that he would clarify the roles and responsibilities for a long-term job, and ask for a decision within the next day or two. But that was not what happened.

As far as I know Jack was not a man of faith, but he was a good businessman. He knew I had a divided heart. I believe that given the potential and significance of the possible future with the company, Jack didn't want just part of me. He wanted to know and be convinced that I was **all in**.

As we sat at the dinner table that night, I explained to Grandmom what had happened the night before as I lay in bed. I then told her about Jack asking me to go to lunch with him, what I was expecting would happen, and what actually occurred. I cannot remember how the conversation evolved from that point, but what I do know is, both of us knew we **really** had to seek the Lord on what to do over the next week.

The exact words we prayed, I also do not know, but they were something like, "Oh God, You are so amazing. We can't believe that Jack would encourage us to go to the Cru training or that while we are there, to make a decision related to our future. We do not know what all of this means, but we want to follow You. We surrender totally to your desires and your will. Please guide us each step of the way so we can fulfill Your plans for us. In Jesus' name, Amen."

Chapter 15

FarFar's Love and Warning

————————⚬————————

I n June prior to our wedding, Grandmom was still finishing two
classes at the University of Buffalo. At the same time, we had
the opportunity to travel with Cru to a Christian gathering for a
reported 75,000 in Dallas, Texas-Explo '72. The timing of the conference was definitely a conflict for Grandmom since she was in
the final weeks of the classes required for graduation. After much
prayer and in faith, Grandmom decided "you have not because
you ask not" (taken from James 4:2) and approached her professors, mentioning that she had a significant opportunity to attend
a conference. Against all odds, they agreed to let her take a week
from classes and go. It was incredible! While there, we had gone
to the booths of dozens of Christian organizations to learn about
their ministries, the training they offered and the opportunities for
service. Back in New Jersey we also became aware of a ministry
to high school students that some Christians near my home were
hoping to start. They had asked us to pray and challenged us to
consider joining their ministry. Consequently, numerous possibilities for the future were on our minds. Though we still weren't sure
of God's ultimate direction for us, we became confident that we
needed to move forward in the application process to attend the

Cru training for new or prospective staff members. We continued to wait on God for direction.

Prior to our departure for California to attend the training with Cru, the love and concern that my dad had for us compelled him to pull me aside one night to talk. As I mentioned before, FarFar was a man of very few words. In fact, apart from talking to me about how to organize and save/spend money, I cannot remember another time when he took the initiative to ask me to discuss something with him. That night, what FarFar said to me blew me away.

He began by saying, "I know you and Char are planning to go out to California for the ministry training. I think you know what my preference would be for your future (he was very aware of the opportunity with the company). But, it is your life, and you have to make your own decisions." Dad, FarFar, in his own way was saying, *I release you from fulfilling my dream. It is your life and you need to fulfill your own dreams.*

What a demonstration of sacrificial love! At the crucial moment when either his life dream would take a significant step towards being fulfilled, or move in what he believed to be the opposite direction, he was saying it was my life, it was my decision.

I was amazed, and will never forget that moment and his act of love.

At the same time, in his love, he didn't want me to make a decision I would later regret. He went on to say, "I don't want you to make this decision without realizing the consequences of your actions. If you go with this organization, you need to realize that you will never again be able to buy a new car with cash." (I had made and saved a lot of money when I worked at the company. As a result, at the end of my sophomore year in college, I was able to buy a brand new car with cash — something rarely done by a college student whose family wasn't wealthy).

"You will never be able to buy a home, you will struggle to provide adequately for your family, and you will not be able to live the way you have become accustomed to living. It is your decision, but you need to realize and weigh the consequences of your decision."

Thanking my dad for caring enough to take the initiative to talk with me and share his concerns, I told him we would not take his words lightly. And we didn't. It was my desire and commitment to "honor my father and my mother" (Deuteronomy 5:16). I told him that I loved and respected him and appreciated all that he and my mom had done for us. At the same time, we believed God was the ultimate provider and that our lives were in His hands.

As Grandmom and I got into the car that October day to begin our trip to California, we were so excited. We didn't know what the Lord had planned for us, but we knew this trip to California would be a significant part of finding out. Along the way, three rather crazy stories occurred, which I will get to in the following chapters, but I wanted to tell you what happened in California right now.

I had taken a month off work and we had traveled all the way across the country. We were about two hours north of Cru headquarters, which back then was located in San Bernardino, CA. As we sat in the car and talked about what to do next, we realized that when we applied for staff training, we were only given a tentative date for it to begin. We had never received a letter of acceptance, nor other crucial information before we left New Jersey. As a result, we not only didn't know specifically when the training began, we also didn't know if we had been accepted to attend the training.

What? How foolish could we be? We were so naïve. We had traveled over 3,000 miles to attend a training for which we hadn't been accepted. Just a slight oversight.

Shaking our heads in disbelief at what we had done, we decided we needed to call Cru headquarters. As I stood in the phone booth, waiting for the call to go through, I felt so stupid. All I could think was, *Oh man, what do we do if we weren't invited to attend the training?* The receptionist transferred me to someone in Human Resources. I was told we were invited for the training (Oh God, thank You), but we were not yet accepted to staff. Acceptance to staff would possibly come after I had some meetings with one of their representatives, and if we decided this was the direction in which God was leading.

How do you spell relief? I spelled it, I-N-V-I-T-E-D to attend staff training.

While at the training, your Grandmom and I constantly prayed, "God, please guide us to know what Your will is for our lives. We don't know for sure if You want us to go into full-time vocational ministry or for me to take the job at the company and for Char to become a nurse. If we go into vocational ministry, we do not know if You want us to go with Cru, with the high school ministry back home, or some other organization. Even if we go with Cru, we don't know what ministry You want us to be in, whether the campus/college ministry or the high school ministry. Please guide us, Lord. We only want to do Your will."

As the days began to pass, we realized that if we went with Cru, we needed to make a ministry focus decision. If we went with the college ministry, there would be one path of training. If we went with the high school ministry, there was a separate training. The decision on the company, Cru, or some other organization wouldn't have to be made for another week, but the decision regarding a training path had to be made now. We prayed, "God, please guide our minds, thoughts, and this decision."

As Grandmom and I talked about it, we realized that whatever the future held, we could benefit from having the Cru training for ministering to high school students. After praying through all of this more, we decided to identify ourselves with the high school training path.

The next week, I had meetings with the Cru representatives, and afterwards we were informed that we would be accepted to staff. It was at this point that the decision on the company or which high school ministry to take had to be made. Once again, going before God, we asked Him to guide our thoughts and decisions. There seemed to be so many decisions linked to next step decisions. Relying on His faithfulness was the source of our hope and confidence.

As we processed what had occurred in the previous weeks, we recognized that a major reason why we were in California attending the Christian training was due to the encouragement of someone who was not spiritually oriented. To us, it seemed very unusual for someone like Jack to encourage us to do this. Jack was also the one who encouraged us to make the decision for our life direction while we were away. As we reflected on what had occurred, we came to two conclusions: 1-we had both truly surrendered to doing whatever our Lord wanted; and 2-we believed that God had cleared the way for us to go into full-time Christian vocational ministry.

Next, we had the issue of which ministry organization to join! So many decisions! It was definitely a journey through questions, with unknown answers, while trusting God to faithfully guide us in His timing. We called the people who had been a part of starting the ministry in New Jersey, asked them to explain their vision more fully, and to let us know what they would have in the form of training for us. Their vision for the ministry would begin in one school in South Jersey, but would ultimately spread throughout the South Jersey region, which was great. However, the degree of training they could provide would be minimal. There was one youth leader associated with Youth for Christ who was willing to help us, but we had heard through other sources that he was exceptionally busy and already over-extended with his time. The other piece of information we received was that they would be willing to provide 50 percent of our salary, and all our ministry expenses. That certainly was an interesting piece of the puzzle.

As we continued to gather information, we became aware that with Cru, both of us would have a personal ministry trainer- a woman for Char, and a man for me. As we started out, our need for good training was a high priority. Whether we stayed with Cru long term, joined another ministry, or after a few years went into a secular job, we knew the training we received would benefit us for a lifetime of serving our Lord. After prayer, our hearts and minds became set on this long-term benefit. We decided to join the high school ministry of Cru.

You may wonder why we shared all the details related to the decisions we faced at this point in our lives. We thought it might be helpful to you for several reasons.

The multiple decisions were simply a part of our journey in following God, which can often be complex.

As we followed the Lord in this process, we spent a significant amount of time, months in fact, not knowing what to do. Most of us don't like it when we are stuck, unable to discern the best decision. We want our answers for direction to be given to us instantaneously. And yet, if that occurred, the muscle of faith wouldn't be developed. It is during the periods of "not knowing," that true faith and dependence upon God are tested and strengthened. The very fact that we do not know or understand what to do compels us to seek Him more, to examine our hearts to ensure complete surrender to Him continues, and to depend on the promises of His Word with greater focus. Promises like:

> Proverbs 3:5,6 "Trust in the LORD with all your heart, And do not lean on your own understanding. In all your ways acknowledge Him, and he will make your paths straight."

> Proverbs 16:9 "The mind of man plans his way, but the LORD directs his steps."

95

> Psalm 37:4-7a "Delight yourself in the LORD; And He will give you the desires of your heart. Commit your way to the LORD, trust also in Him, and He will do it. He will bring forth your righteousness as the light and your judgment as the noonday. Rest in the Lord and wait patiently for Him."

> Psalm 119:105 "Your Word is a lamp to my feet, and a light to my path."

Often when we walk in the dark, we can only see what is immediately ahead of us. But God's desire is to guide us down the path, His path, one step at a time.

Finally, after we surrendered to whatever God wanted, and trusted Him to guide our thoughts, our information gathering, and our interactions, we could look back and see how God led us towards each decision. Thus we can say, "Great is His faithfulness!"

But wait, I think I mentioned earlier that we had three crazy stories that occurred on the trip to California. One involves life and death; another, possibly angels; and the third is just a funny situation.

Chapter 16

"WAS THAT DEMONIC?"

———————⟨×⟩———————

A s we departed for the Cru training, we had to travel across
the country, from the east coast to the west coast. We had a
great time driving across the states of Pennsylvania, Ohio, Indiana,
Illinois, and Missouri.

One observation we noticed as we drove on I-70 in Kansas is
how the road stretches in front of you for miles into the horizon.
As a result, we easily observed a guy hitchhiking about a mile
down the road.

Immediately, I asked Char, "Should we pick him up?"

Having been a hitchhiker myself, I appreciated it when someone
would stop and pick me up. Grandmom was a bit hesitant. She could
still recall giving a speech on *"The Evils of Hitchhiking"* during
a speech competition when she was in high school. Little did she
know that she would later be married because of an "un-named"
hitchhiker.

Reluctantly, Grandmom agreed. Touching the brakes and
slowing down, we pulled over to the side of the road. Throwing a
bag into the back seat, a young guy, approximately twenty years
old, climbed in. The back seat and floor board were already packed
high, but he didn't seem to mind the "lift"! He was a bit unkempt.

He had long dark hair that fell to his shoulders (not that unusual in the early '70s) and it looked like he hadn't shaved for a few days.

I know you grandchildren have never hitchhiked before, and your mom will be very glad to hear me say, "Times have changed!" Thus, you should **never** hitchhike, nor should you ever pick up hitchhikers! Be sure you remember this. Moms (especially my daughters), are you glad I mentioned this strong admonition?

That being said, the normal conversation when a hitchhiker gets picked up is you ask, "What's your name?" "Where are you coming from?" and "Where are you going?" I cannot remember his name, but for this story, let's call him John. Nor do I recall where he was going. What I can vividly remember is where he said he came from.

He responded by saying that he had spent a few weeks at a commune.

At this time in the 1970s, New Age-oriented people sometimes decided to live in a setting where several families or groups of individuals lived together. Thus, instead of living as a normal family, dad, mom, and children, a larger group of people would live on a farm, or in a group of homes next to each other. In some ways, it might have been similar to the New Testament church in Acts, where people were selling their individual possessions, bringing them to the apostles, who then distributed things to the saints. However, in other ways, the communes could be very different from the early church. Often, the use of drugs, the practice of eastern religions, the worship of Satan, and/or other practices occurred. Not always, but many times, that was the case. In addition to the normal extended "family" of the commune, other individuals with similar persuasions and practices could freely drop in and live at the commune for periods of time. This was what John had done.

From his speech, it seemed that John might still have been high on drugs, and as he talked about his days at the commune, it was obvious that either some practices of eastern mysticism or Satan worship had occurred. My immediate thought was, *Wow, this guy really needs to know the hope, love, and power of the Lord*. After listening to his story for a while, I began sharing my story with him. I shared how for a while I had rejected Christianity, but then ran into other students whose lives had been transformed through a personal relationship with Jesus Chr—

Ahhhhhhh!

The rear of our car began spinning to the left, pulling us over the left lane and shoulder of the highway. Across the grassy median we continued as I attempted to get the car under control without success. The car proceeded onto the two lanes of oncoming traffic on the other side of I-70. A large semi-truck came into view. Somehow the car reversed direction and we went back into the grassy median area of the highway. We came to a stop.

Stunned, the three of us sat in the car unable to move, trying to understand what had just happened. We were in one piece, we didn't hit any other cars, we avoided the semi. We, I thought, were okay. Slowly, we all confirmed this to be true. We got out of the car to see if there was damage. One wheel rim was bent and the tire was losing air. It seemed we might be able to drive on it for a short period of time. With flashers blinking, we drove up from the median, across the two lanes, over to the far shoulder of the road. Fortunately, less than a mile away, we saw an exit for a town. We drove towards the small town and quickly saw a car repair station. When I walked into the station an attendant immediately came out to look at the car. He said he could get us a new wheel rim and tire, and we could be on our way in a couple of hours.

I returned to the car. Char and John had continued to sit in it, still recovering from the shock of knowing that we could have died fifteen minutes earlier. By now, I had recovered sufficiently to be able to think coherently. We talked about the life and death experience with John, and asked him if he wanted to wait with us until the car was repaired.

John said, "No, thanks. I think I'll keep going on my own."

Grandmom and I got something to eat in a nearby restaurant as we waited for the car to be repaired. As we talked, we reflected on what had occurred. I knew it had begun to rain slightly as we pulled back onto the road with John in the car. After long spells without rain, oil can build up on the road, thus making it slick until enough rain comes and washes the oil off. Yet we were on a totally straight stretch of highway. I didn't have to turn the steering wheel at all. John had obviously been involved with drugs and possibly spirit worship prior to getting into the car. Had he brought with him a demonic spirit, who, when he began to hear the victorious name of Jesus Christ, threw a fit and threw our car into a spin? It was certainly an interesting scenario.

We really do not know. What we **do** know is that Jesus Christ preserved our lives, enabled our car to be repaired without difficulty, while also providing John with some words of truth in the midst of a potentially life-ending experience.

Chapter 17

"Did We Meet Angels?"

———————✕———————

After driving all day, by 9pm we were ready to find a KOA or other campsite and go to sleep. Mile, after mile, after mile passed, and all we could see was more barbed-wire fences and tumbleweed in eastern Colorado. Having left I-70, we headed southwest on Rt. 24, a two-lane road towards Colorado Springs. As I felt exhaustion and sleepiness settling in, we saw a sign: *Bible Church — Right three miles.*

I said to Char, "Honey, why don't we drive to the church and see if we can pitch our tent on its lawn?" It seemed a better option than waking up in a field with cows staring down at us. Also tired from the long day of travel, she agreed and we proceeded down the dirt road. After driving for what seemed like a lot more than three miles, I began looking at my odometer. We traveled for another three miles without seeing a single structure. I was ready to turn around, when we saw a light up ahead. It turned out that it wasn't a church, but rather a ranch home. Since it had its front light on, I decided to go and ask them where the church might be.

The woman who came to the door, in a friendly manner said, "Oh yes. It's three miles down the road."

Char and I had both looked at the sign for the church on the road, and we had both read three miles. If we had seen thirteen miles, we never would have gone that far out of our way. But being this far we decided to continue…three more miles!

As we arrived at the church building, we noticed lights lit in the basement. I thought if someone was there, it would be better to get permission before we pitched our tent. I walked to the doors and rang the bell. A man, I guess in his forties, appeared. After briefly explaining who we were and where we were going, I asked if it would be okay if we pitched our tent out by the car.

He said, "Sure."

I thanked him and walked back to Grandmom who was still in the car.

While we were unpacking the trunk and getting out the tent, the man reappeared. Kindly he commented, "We have an extra double bed downstairs, why don't you come inside and sleep there?"

I looked at Char, she seemed agreeable, and so I said, "That would be great!"

As we went down the stairs, we were greeted by a warm, friendly woman. The church was a new church plant, and the minister and his wife were living in the basement of the church, with their two children (who were already in bed), until the church grew large enough to also provide them with a home. They asked us to sit down and have something to drink before we went to bed. It was an encouraging time in which we were able to share our stories of coming to know Christ and our desire to glorify Him. Around 11pm, we went to our small bedroom, closed our eyes, and we were out.

The next thing we knew, the aroma of fresh baked bread, bacon, coffee, and other welcoming aromas filled the air. We got dressed and went into the kitchen. The wife greeted us with, "Please sit down, and have some breakfast." What a feast we had: pancakes, eggs, bacon, fresh muffins, orange juice, coffee. The works! As we ate, she told us that the pastor and their two children had left earlier in the morning, since he drove the school bus each morning.

After the fantastic breakfast, she told us it would take us a while before we could get on the road. With curiosity, I asked her why. Apparently in the middle of the night, it began to rain and then the temperature dropped forty degrees and below freezing in a matter of minutes. An "ice storm" had occurred! I had never heard of such a thing.

Going out to our car, I couldn't believe my eyes. It was covered with one continuous sheet of ice! You couldn't even see the space between the doors and the frame of the car. I walked back to the church to borrow some tools, since I couldn't get into the trunk to get mine. With a hammer and flat head screwdriver, I began chipping away at the ice around the driver's side door. The ice from all four sides of the door had to be chipped away before the door would open. Once the door was free from the ice and opened, I started the engine and put on the heater and defroster, hoping the heat would begin a second process of ice removal. An hour later we were giving a huge thanks and a good-bye to the wife, asking her to let the pastor know how much we appreciated their kindness and love. Before we left, Char got the address of the church and their names from the wife.

Weeks later, after we returned to FarFar's and Nana's house following our training, we were surprised to find in our pile of mail, the thank you card we had sent to the pastor and his wife. We had sent it to them soon after we arrived in California for the training. The Post Office comment said, "Address unknown." This seemed strange to us, because we had gotten the information directly from the pastor's wife.

Not knowing what else to do, we did nothing.

In June, one-and-a-half years later, we were traveling to our national staff training being held in Fort Collins, CO. We had some extra time to visit parts of Colorado. As we reflected on our previous trip through Colorado, our thoughts turned to the pastor and his wife and how kind they had been to us. Plus, they had never received our thank you note. We decided to stop by to see them!

There are many things I am not good at, but one thing I am good at relates to directions, and a sense of where I am when it comes to roads, mileage, etc. We knew we had traveled on Rt. 24 to get to Colorado Springs. We also knew the amount of time we had traveled after leaving I-70. Definitely within a fifteen-minute radius, I could tell you where we turned for the church. As we went to the place where the sign should have been, we could not find it. We drove back and forth several times without seeing the sign. Finally, we stopped at the closest ranch and went up to the door.

I mentioned the church to the rancher. His response was, "I've lived here a long time, and there has never been a Bible church out here." Bewildered, I walked back to the car and Char.

We got the address from the woman and mailed the thank you within two weeks. The letter was returned, stating an unknown address three weeks later. And now, one-and-a-half years later, a rancher told us the church building never existed. What do you do with that information?

Where was the building? Who did we meet that night? Who made us that fantastic breakfast, and saved us from freezing in our tent from the ice storm?

Did we meet angels? I don't know. But it is one of the things I'd like to find out when I get to heaven.

Chapter 18

"What was That?"

We were camping at a state park in California right on the Pacific Ocean. The weather was fantastic. The stars were beautiful, the smell of the ocean air was inviting, and the ocean provided its usual peaceful yet powerful sound of the waves.

In contrast to this wonderful welcome, the warning sign at the park restrooms suggested we could also encounter some other not so easily welcomed entities. Warnings related to rattlesnakes, bears, and other ominous animals encouraged us to watch where we were stepping, and not to take **any food** into our tent.

That night, for some reason, our usual system of getting everything out of the car and into the tent didn't seem to be functioning that well. We thought we were just about ready for bed and realized we forgot something. Char offered to go to the car to get it. After she returned, we realized we had forgotten something else. This time I offered to go. As I got to the car, over in the trees I heard this loud **thrashing** sound. I froze, afraid to budge.

It stopped, and then five seconds later, it began again. I couldn't believe the sound of the bushes being run over! The noise gradually moved away, and cautiously I returned to the tent. After a few minutes, in as calm a voice as I could muster, I said, "Honey, are you sure we were careful not to bring any food into the tent?"

She said, "Yes, I am sure."

With that, we settled into our sleeping bags and had our normal time of prayer before we went to sleep. The next morning, as we finished breakfast and packed things back into the car, I said to Char, "I didn't say anything to you last night because I didn't want you to be scared, but when I went out to the car, I heard this unbelievable thrashing in the bushes. It must have been a bear."

"I heard the same thing when I went out to the car." She was chuckling when she said that. Apparently she had been a bit nervous when I had left the tent and anxiously awaited my return. We both had a good laugh and appreciated the fact that both of us deliberately chose not to mention it, because we didn't want the other to be worried.

I think, however, our all-time best camping story comes next! It wasn't on our trip to California, but a couple years later.

Chapter 19

"Get Out of the Tent and Into the Car."

—————————∝—————————

We had finished our first year of ministry to high school students in Del City, Oklahoma. Prior to going to our graduate level biblical studies and national staff training, we had a week to camp in the beautiful mountains of Colorado. We traveled to the San Juan Mountains of Southwest Colorado and found a beautiful camping spot right near a swift-running stream. It was a beautiful but cool June evening. As we put out the fire, the coolness quickly turned to cold and seemed to settle into our tent.

Crawling into our sleeping bags, we tried to get warm as we said our prayers. We kissed as we always did after our prayers, and I turned to lie on my side.

As I closed my eyes, the thought came to my mind: *Get out of the tent and into the car.* Considering it an absurd thought, I again tried to put my mind and body at ease, and sleep. Immediately, the thought returned, *Get out of the tent and into the car.* Again, I tried to discard the thought, saying to myself, "Just go to sleep." But the thought, *"Get out of the tent and into the car"* would not leave.

Concerned, I said to Grandmom, "Honey, I know that this will sound strange, but I can't get this thought out of my head: *'Get out of the tent and into the car.'"* She responded, "That **is** strange. Just roll over and go to sleep." And, that's exactly what I did… at least the first part of rolling over.

As I lay there, the thought again returned: *Get out of the tent and into the car. Get out of the tent and into the car. Get out of the tent and into the car.* After five minutes of this, I was really troubled.

"Honey, I know it sounds crazy, and I know you do not want to, but I can't get this thought out of my mind. I don't know if it is the Lord putting this thought in my head or not, but I think we should get out of the tent and into the car."

"You are right, it sounds crazy," she said. "I'm just starting to get warm, and I really don't want to get out of this sleeping bag. It's cold out! Please, can't you just go to sleep?" Normally, Grandmom is very agreeable and willing to follow my suggestions. But with that as her response, I really did try to go to sleep… one more time.

As I turned over and tried once again to go to sleep, all that filled my mind was, *Get out of the tent and into the car. Get out of the tent and into the car. Get out of the tent and into the car.* This thought, crazy or not, would not go away. Finally, I turned over and said in a very strong way, "Char, I know that you do not want to get out of the sleeping bag and tent. But I cannot get this thought out of my mind, and right now, we need to get out of this tent and into the car! Come on."

"Are you kidding me? Do we have to?" she replied.

I was up, getting ready to move to the car. Reluctantly, she climbed out of her bag. Grandmom got into the back seat of the car, and I got into the front seat. We both tried to get comfortable and warm.

I said, "I love you," and blew her a kiss over the seat good night. *Ahhhh…* I was finally able to sleep.

The wind howled, rain came down in torrents, trees were blowing to their sides, then hail began to hit the bushes, the top of the car, and the tent. I couldn't believe it.

"I guess the Lord knew this was coming," I said out loud. The storm continued about half an hour. It was wild!

In the morning, we got up and looked around. Branches were down on the ground. There was a slight tear in the tent, and everything we had left in the tent was soaked. Drenched! The tent leaned slightly towards one corner, leaving a good-sized puddle of water. What a mess!

Before breakfast, we hung a rope and put what was wet on it to dry. We opened the flaps of the tent and mopped up the water.

At breakfast as we reflected on what had occurred, I thought and prayed, "Lord, we wouldn't have died if we had stayed in the tent. But thanks for caring so much about us, for wanting to be so real to us, to let us know that a storm was coming. Thanks for loving us enough to put these words in my head, *'Get out of the tent and into the car.'*"

Chapter 20

"Oh God, What am I to Do?"

———⟨⟩———

Total brokenness.
Absolutely lost in terms of what to do.
Crying to God from the deepest part of my soul.

There have been several times in my life when this has been my reality. The first time was when I asked your Grandmom to marry me, struggled with whether I had really blown it, and whether or not I needed to cut off our engagement and relationship.

This chapter tells of another one of those times. Every time I think about it, the impact of this situation affects me deep within my soul.

As we joined the staff of Cru, one thing certain in our minds was that our hearts truly had surrendered to Christ as the Lord and the Master of our lives. We lived in a way that acknowledged God as being:

Omniscient – He knows everything! Which is a lot more than we know about ourselves, our circumstances, His purposes, His plans for the world, and our individual lives. Psalm 139:1-3 says,

O, LORD, You have searched me and known me.
You know when I sit down and when I rise up;
You understand my thought from afar.
You scrutinize my path and my lying down,

And are intimately acquainted with all my ways."

Our Creator, Purpose Giver – He gave each of us our unique DNA, which in part enables us to fulfill His purposes for our lives. Psalm 139:13: "For You formed my inward parts; You wove me in my mother's womb." As we are born again, we receive additional gifting. 1 Corinthians 12:7 says, "But to each one is given the manifestation of the Spirit for the common good." And as it says in Ephesians 2:10, "For we are His workmanship, created in Christ Jesus for good works, which God prepared beforehand so that we would walk in them."

All Powerful – No one and nothing can inhibit God from leading us and guiding us in fulfilling His purposes for our lives. As He said to Abram in Genesis 17:1, 2, "I am God Almighty. Walk before me, and be blameless. I will establish My covenant between Me and you."

Faithful – He will continue to faithfully lead us and provide for us, despite the size of the barriers, the hindrances, or the bleakness of the situation before us. 1Thessalonians 5:24 declares: "Faithful is He who calls you, and He also will bring it to pass." Psalm 33:4 says, "For the word of the LORD is upright; and all His work is done in faithfulness."

Belief in these four attributes or characteristics of God enabled us to continue to endure through the extremely challenging first effort of raising our initial financial support as staff with Cru.

In my hometown, we knew very few committed Christians who wanted to join us as we followed the Lord. Grandmom's rural hometown of 2,000 residents had limited resources. The total number of times we ended up with no other possible individuals, families, or churches to call to see if they would be interested in our ministry was lost due to its frequency. But then we would get one more referral, and continue the search for those whom God desired to participate with us in ministry. Months and months went by with little to show for our efforts. The support goal we were trying to raise was about $1,065 per month, to cover the salary for a staff couple at $510 a month, with the remainder for ministry expenses, health benefits, pension, overseas ministries, and other overhead/administrative office costs.

Progress was so slow that in a phone call for encouragement from the high school ministry regional director, he said, "I can't believe that you guys are still hanging on and haven't given up." Despite the challenges, we persevered, never doubting that we were following the will of the Lord. We felt that in His way, and in His timing, He would provide.

Gradually by mid-summer, we got to about the $800 per month level of commitments, and due to some one-time gifts had several thousand dollars in our account. What occurred then would not be permitted now, but in July the regional director gave us another call and said, "Why don't you come to Oklahoma City? If your support runs into trouble, you can come down to Dallas. I'll see if I can line you up with some possible ministry partners." Excitedly, we said, "Okay." We were ready and eager to begin this next adventure!

Even today, I can picture us driving away from my parent's home where we had been living for several months. The next step of our journey of faith, with a loaded thirteen-foot U-Haul truck and our car in tow was in motion. We were so excited to finally begin our ministry to students, meet our staff team, and see what God was going to do. The first weeks and months of ministry were exciting. Two single men and two single women were a part of the great team we joined. We would be reaching out to students at several high schools just east of Oklahoma City, whose administrations wanted the positive influence in the schools that we could bring. We had completely free access to walk into the schools during the day, eat lunch in the cafeteria, meet with students during study halls, and have programs after school. Many of the Christian students in the schools wanted to gather around us and introduce us to their friends. It was a great!

But as these great things were occurring, simultaneously our personal financial account began to plummet. We began receiving fewer donations each month, no more one-time gifts, and by October we were in the maximum deficit of $510. It gets a little tricky and confusing, but basically, after you reach maximum deficit, you can only receive as your salary (money to buy food, pay the rent and other expenses) the funds that remain after taxes and the additional fees are deducted, without exceeding the deficit limit of $510. I gave a call to Gary, our regional director, shared what was happening, and he arranged for me to go down to Dallas in November.

Another important piece of information is why we couldn't simply raise the financial support we needed in Oklahoma City. In the early '70s, some people went to different parts of the country, spoke in churches, said they were part of Cru, and that they were planning to start a Cru ministry at a nearby college or university. They received money from the churches and disappeared with the cash. After a while, the churches who had heard nothing about the ministry began to ask, *Where are those Cru staff we supported?* Unable to find anything about them at the universities, they called Cru headquarters. It was soon discovered that they were never on staff with Cru, but were imposters. In fact, this exact thing had happened in Elmira, New York, forty-five minutes from Char's home. When we came and wanted to share about our ministry with Cru, a lot of churches didn't want to talk to us. As a result of the imposters, Cru established a policy whereby no one could seek ministry partners in the area of their ministry until they had ministered there for at least one year. Consequently, we were not permitted to establish a ministry partner team in Oklahoma City.

When I arrived in Dallas, Gary gave me the names of about twenty people. As I called them, explained that my wife and I were from New York and New Jersey, and that we were involved in a high school ministry in Oklahoma City, there wasn't a lot of interest. Let me briefly explain. First, we were not homegrown Texans. Second, those in Texas knew there were a lot of Christian financial resources in Oklahoma City. And third, even though they were Christians, a lot of statehood and sport team rivalry was retained by those from Texas and Oklahoma that added interesting dynamics. At least that was true back then. Providing the explanation as to why we couldn't have ministry partners in Oklahoma didn't overcome those obstacles. At the end of my trip to Dallas, we had received one commitment of $10 per month and that never came into our account.

During this time, each month we sent a letter to those back east about the exciting things God was doing in the lives of students, while also sharing the increasing financial need. Unfortunately, donations continued to decline through November.

As December arrived, I still had hope that things would turn around. Historically, because of Christmas and the end-of-the-year contributions that people like to give, December is the month in which the greatest amount of charitable contributions are received. Thus, I hoped that it would be a strong month for us. Unfortunately, my hopes were dashed. On January 10th, when we received the donations total for the month of December, we had only received $310 into our account. That is the amount *before* taxes and *before* the other deductions! The paycheck itself was around $200.

In late January, as concern about our financial situation escalated, Grandmom began to feel very nauseous and sick. A really bad case of the flu, or so we thought. Unfortunately, it persisted! She went to our doctor. He and his wife had become special friends to us through the church we had joined. He wanted to do some "special" tests before he would do an x-ray. A pregnancy test might have been mentioned, but your Grandmom was in somewhat of a daze and it's hard to say for certain. The fact that a pregnancy test was taken was later confirmed.

I can recall hearing the phone ring, knowing that it was probably the doctor's report regarding the pregnancy test. His instincts were correct. It wasn't the flu. A new life had begun and in nine months we would have a baby! This was a complete shock to us, because at this point, we hadn't planned to begin a family yet. Inside I was thankful, but also more concerned about our financial situation than ever before.

Why? Let me tell you.

Though Cru had health insurance, it did not include maternity (having a baby) coverage in 1974. You could cover the costs through a medical withdrawal from your personal account, but this was of no help to us, since our account was at the maximum deficit! By this time, your Grandmom was **very** sick. She was nauseous twenty-four hours a day and having dry heaves, since there was nothing left in her stomach to throw up. Brushing her teeth made her gag! Sitting up in bed, or trying to walk to the bathroom, made the room spin. She felt miserable and unfortunately I could do little to help.

So, to summarize the situation: My wife was extremely sick, our financial needs had now increased dramatically, and I was stuck. Since she was sick, I couldn't go back east. I couldn't raise contributions in Oklahoma. Dallas had been a bust. And the letters sent back east were accomplishing nothing. It seemed that the only thing I could do was pray for a miracle. So that is what I did.

With this as my reality, I can vividly remember going to our apartment mailbox on February 10, the day we received the end of the month check for January. As I retrieved the blue envelope from the box and walked inside our apartment, I said, "Lord, I do not know what it says in this envelope, but I know that You are all-powerful. If You want, You can even change everything it says right now. I again ask You for a miracle."

As I opened the envelope, I took a deep breath and continued in prayer.

What do you think I saw?

The grand total of contributions that we received for the month was $275.

My heart broke. All I could say was, "Oh God. Oh God. What am I to do? What am I to do?" I went over to the chair where I had my daily time with the Lord, and said again, "God, what am I to do? Char is so sick she can't get out of bed. I can't raise donations in Oklahoma City. Dallas was a complete waste of time and money. I can't go back east because Char is sick. Despite three or four distress letters back home, there has been no response. **God, what am I to do?**"

Groaning within, I grasped my Bible, not even knowing what to do with it. I simply flipped it open as I continued to shake my head in despair. Then, I looked down at the scriptures, and this is what I saw:

" 'Bring the whole tithe into the storehouse, so that there may be food in My house, and test Me now in this', says the LORD of hosts, 'if I will not open for you the windows of heaven and pour out for you a blessing until it overflows.' " Malachi 3:10

"**What**?" I said. "**What did You say**?" I re-read the words, a second and then a third time.

Then I said, "**Well God, You have the test!**"

At that moment, I was **overwhelmed** with a sense of peace. Instantly I knew within, God was going to do a miracle. I saw God's promise. Despite the short paychecks, we had continued to give the first fruits of our paycheck to God.

I will share more about this later, but as a new couple we had sought God's wisdom in giving back to Him what we had received, and felt that He had led us to give more than a tithe of 10 percent.

Almost immediately I felt compelled to share with our ministry partners what had happened. Thus, probably for the fourth time I sent an update, i.e., distress letter. Only this time, I didn't say that we were trusting God for a miracle, I said I knew God was going to do a miracle. And, I truly did believe He was about to do something miraculous in our midst.

As I went to the mailbox the next month to retrieve the blue envelope, I took it, walked through the door once again, and said, "God, I do not know what You did, but I thank You for it whatever it was." I tore open the envelope, pulled out the sheets of paper, and what do you think I saw? Tell me!

That month, instead of the $310 or the $275 that we had received for the previous two months, we received $2,185. I began to gasp with thanksgiving, rejoicing in God's faithfulness. (Even now as I write this, my eyes are tearing up in emotion. It was an incredible, life changing moment.) "God," I said, "You are soooooooo **good**. You are soooooooo **faithful**. Thank You, thank You, thank You!"

But the pouring out until it "overflows" did not stop there.

A few days after we received our first full paycheck of $510 in four months, Char had her second appointment with her obstetrician (baby doctor). During her first visit, she was told that since we didn't have health coverage for the costs, each month we would have to pay one-ninth of the cost. Since she would now be going for her second appointment, we would have to pay two-ninths of the cost. We scraped our money together, virtually eliminating our savings. As she walked up to the receptionist after her appointment to pay, she said her name and the receptionist said, "Oh, you don't owe anything."

Surprised, Grandmom said, "You must be looking at the wrong name, because we haven't paid anything."

The receptionist said, "What is your name again?" She looked down again at the account and replied, "No I was correct. You do not owe anything. In fact, the bill for your pregnancy has been paid in full."

Grandmom stood there in a state of shock. She didn't know what to say, except, "Thank you."

We later found out that one day, our doctor friend was treating patients and the thought popped into his mind, "Go pay the obstetrician's bill for Char and Ron." Initially, he just went, "Hmmm," but as he continued through the day, the thought kept coming back to him. Thus after work that day, he drove over to the other doctor's office and paid our entire bill.

We had not mentioned a word about our financial situation over the previous four months to anyone in Oklahoma. Doing that would have violated Cru policy. However, we had no control over what God might say to someone. God just decided to do the talking for us.

The next month we received $1,500 in our account. After all these years, trust me when I tell you the rounded off amounts. It is not likely I will **ever** forget them! It was a **huge** blessing and unforgettable intervention of our heavenly Father.

We had been given another opportunity to surrender **all** to Him. Those two months of contributions got us through the rest of the spring months and through our summer expenses. Upon our return from our summer assignment in August, I was able within Cru policy to find ministry partners in Oklahoma. In eight weeks, over $700 of solid monthly support was pledged. Our needs for our lives, ministry, and our new baby had been met.

God had once again demonstrated **His faithfulness!**

Chapter 21

"Oh No! I Didn't Say That, Did I?"

After two years in Oklahoma, we transferred to the college ministry of Cru and were assigned to minister at West Chester University, which is outside of Philadelphia. One night, for a guys' relationship building event, we decided to go to a Phillies baseball game. You know how much of a Phillies fan I am, though maybe not quite the "Philly Phanatic" that my dad was.

That night in late September, the game had about five rain delays. Being the end of the season, the umps wanted it to count as a complete game. Thus, when the rain died down a little, out would come the players until the next downpour. But college guys can enjoy themselves at a sporting event regardless of the environment, so we decided to stay as long as it took. The game finally ended a little after midnight. By the time we got to the cars and drove back to West Chester, it was about 1:15am. My car was parked on the road that ran along the outskirts of the campus. As I walked over to unlock my car door, a little Volkswagon bug drove up alongside me.

My thought was that it was probably some guys needing directions or something like that. I walked over to the car, ducked my head to look in and saw 3 men, and then...

There before my eyes was a gun pointing straight at me.

My first thought was, *Ah, it's probably fake*. But as I stared at it, ten inches from my head, I quickly realized this was solid steel.

The guy in the front seat was yelling at me, "You got any money? You got any money?"

My second quick thought was a silent prayer, *Oh God, help me*.

Again, the guy with the gun barked, "You got any money?"

Then I couldn't believe what happened. I responded to the guy in a sarcastic voice saying, "Well I have a few pennies, but it isn't worth that."

In the next split second and silently I said, *Oh no! I didn't say that, did I?* I was shocked, but so was the twenty-something kid with a gun at my head. In fact, he was so surprised he didn't know what to do, or what to say. He couldn't believe that someone would get sarcastic with him, when he was pointing a gun at his head.

After a pregnant pause, he said, "Well, okay, get out of here."

Slowly, I backed up and then ducked behind my car.

I was ready to get their license plate as they drove away, but they put the car in reverse and backed down the street until they were too far away for me to see their plate. (In Pennsylvania there is only a license plate on the rear of the car, not the front.)

They did a U-turn and took off. Immediately I knew I needed to report what happened. I jumped into my car and drove to the women's dorm, where I knew a security guard was stationed all night. I walked into the dorm, went to the guard, and began to tell him the story.

But he interrupted me! "Excuse me, stop. Where did you say your car was, and where were you standing?"

I couldn't believe he interrupted me without getting more of the details of what happened. I responded, "I was on New street, where my car was parked."

With that, he said, "I don't need to hear anymore. That is out of our jurisdiction, you will need to talk to the West Chester Police. You can wait inside in the lounge or outside. I'll call them."

I felt a bit put off. After all, someone had just put a gun to my head! But there was nothing I could do but wait.

Fresh air sounded like a good idea, so I went outside and sat down on the steps. I was feeling relatively calm, or so I thought.

All of a sudden it felt like my left arm was shaking inside and rattling back and forth. Surprised, I looked down to see if it was moving. The arm was completely still, but the sensation that something was going crazy inside my arm continued. Without realizing it, I apparently was in a slight state of shock.

Finally a uniformed policeman and a plain-clothes detective arrived. They asked me some questions and then asked me to come down to the police station to help recreate a sketch of the guy pointing the gun at me. I followed the police to the station, went in and spent the next hour flipping through different facial parts to attain the desired look. It was tougher than I thought it should have been. I think my eyes were so fixed on the barrel of that gun, I didn't look much at the guy's face, and yet his vague face can still somewhat haunt me.

Returning home, I walked as silently as possible into our bedroom around 3:30am. I was hoping I could slip into bed without waking Grandmom. No such luck.

As soon as I was halfway into bed, she said, "What's wrong, what happened?"

I said, "How did you know something happened?"

She responded, "I don't know, I just know."

I quickly gave her a shortened version of the night, and we went to sleep.

Three weeks later, I got a call from the police department. They wanted me to come down to the station for a line-up of the guy they wanted to nail for the attempted robbery and assault charges. As the guys lined up, the man who held a gun at me was not there. The officers tried to get me to point out one man in particular. This surprised me, since that is not legal. The guy they were trying to nail might have been one of the other two guys in the car that night, but the only face I saw was the guy with the gun.

I have two thoughts as I reflect on this situation. First, God graciously protected me in this life-threatening moment. My second thought is a word of encouragement. Don't ever get sarcastic with someone who has a gun ten inches from your head!

Chapter 22

FAITH DEVASTATED – 300 STUDENTS IN THREE YEARS

———————◅∽▻———————

The Cru leadership had challenged me to be the director of a campus ministry for the first time in my life. In some ways, I was excited about the opportunity. However, I also felt completely inadequate for the job of raising up a movement of students committed to glorifying God.

Prior to moving to Delaware, I made my first visit to the University of Delaware in April. Immediately, I became burdened to fulfill what God wanted to see happen amongst the students. Due in part to my personality and being a goal-motivated guy, I began praying, "God, what do You want me to believe You for at this university? What do You want me to trust You to do?"

When we arrived, the ministry at the University of Delaware was small. About twenty-five students attended our first weekly meeting of the year. Though we began to take some good steps forward, particularly related to prayer, plans for the weekly meetings, and outreaches, it wasn't until about eight months after I began praying, "God, what do You want me to trust You to do?" that the vision began to crystallize in my mind. Initially, I kept what I was thinking to myself, desiring to consider it in prayer for several weeks before sharing it with anyone. But the more I prayed, the more the sense that "this" was what God wanted me to trust Him to do strengthened.

At Delaware, they had a 4-1-4 semester system. What that meant was that the first semester occurred from September through December. Then in January, a one-month term was provided, when students could take one or two classes, or just take time off. Finally, a second full semester took place from February through the first week in May. By January 1, I was convinced that God had given me the vision to trust Him to see a movement of 300 students in three years. To introduce this vision to the students, I planned to give a talk at our weekly meeting about King Jehoshaphat, who trusted God for a miraculous deliverance from his enemies, the Moabites, Ammonites, and Meunites. (2 Chronicles 20:1-12) Though Jehoshaphat was scared and felt helpless, he stood firm against the most challenging and intimidating circumstances, praying, "O our God, will You not judge them? For we are powerless before this great multitude who are coming against us; nor do we know what to do, but our eyes are on You." 2 Chronicles 20:12 I wanted us as a beginning movement to realize 3 things: 1- We are powerless in our own strength to change lives; 2- at this point in time, we really didn't know what to do; and 3- we needed to fix our eyes on God and trust Him to guide us.

As I was on my way to the meeting that night, I was so excited. Then I saw how many students were in the room. I had never been to a Delaware meeting in January before. Since a significant percentage of students chose not to take classes during the January term, many were not on campus. That night, there weren't twenty-five or thirty-five students there. Only seventeen students came to the meeting.

Immediately the wrestling match began in my mind. Thoughts were flooding in and out:

Would it be better to wait to share what God had put on my heart until second semester when more students would be there?

Are you so crazy, that you would share with only seventeen students, a vision to trust God for 300 in three years?

They will think you are absolutely nuts.

You will lose any measure of credibility or respect that you have developed over the last four months.

But this is what God put on my heart, I mentally argued back. *This is what I thought He wanted me to share tonight.*

But there are only seventeen students!

Back and forth my thoughts went as other aspects of the meeting were taking place before I got up to speak.

Finally, I made a decision.

I decided to "Go for it." I determined that I would rather be seen as an idiot and viewed as crazy, than to shrink back from sharing what God had put on my heart. They could call me stupid, but I wasn't going to be a hypocrite in faith and fail to share what God had put on my heart after nine months of praying, "God, what do You want me, want us, to trust You to do?"

To this day, I do not know what the students thought after they walked out of the meeting that night in January. What I do know is, that night was the beginning of seeing God do an amazing work amongst the students at the University of Delaware. Dependence on prayer, trusting God to move, to do the miraculous, to save students, to raise up leaders, became characteristic of the movement. And the vision of faith and trust in a miraculous God was seen as the foundation for all that we did.

Over the next two-and-a-half years, God did His work. By spring semester after two years, about 200 students were involved.

However, I felt we needed something big for God to use to get us to the 300. Over the previous two years, I had asked Josh McDowell to come to the University of Delaware twice. Josh was and continues to this day to be a much sought after, gifted, and challenging speaker. He turned me down both times. I thought that if I asked him again, I would get the same response. As I prayed and thought about it, an idea came to my mind. Josh would probably turn me down the next ten times I asked. He is an extremely busy man with travelling, speaking and writing. But I bet if he got letters from 100 students, over a month's time, asking him to prayerfully consider coming to Delaware, he would change his mind.

With that in mind, I decided to talk to one of our student leaders, Chris. He was a natural, fun-loving, encouraging, people-gathering leader in the movement.

I went to him and said, "Chris, I'd like to ask you to pray about taking on a significant responsibility. The outcome could have a huge impact here in opening doors for God's work and seeing the movement reach the 300 goal by next January. I have asked Josh McDowell to come to Delaware twice, and he turned me down both times. But, if he heard from 100 of the students involved with the movement over a month's time, I think he might come. I want you to go before God, and ask Him if He would want you to lead this effort. I think this needs to be totally student-led. Thus, I would not be involved at all except if you need some advice. This would be your baby. Will you pray about it?"

Chris agreed to pray and several days later told me that he was in.

I was so thankful and excited. I don't think I did a thing after that. Chris simply took the idea and ran with it. Over the next several weeks, every day, Josh received between four and seven letters from students from Delaware, sharing what we were believing God to do, and asking if he would come be a part of it. Josh didn't last a month. In fact, after three weeks God had done enough in his heart that his office gave me a call and said he wanted to change his schedule in the fall so he could come! We arranged a date for him to speak for three consecutive nights during the first week of November.

From my limited perspective, that was the perfect timing. We would have finished the initial thrust of reaching out to freshmen, while having time to prepare students involved in our movement, as well as key students from other Christian organizations on how to invite their friends, and how to share their faith, etc. It would also give us time after Josh's talk to have follow-up conversations with all the interested students and begin to integrate them into the movement before the end of the semester.

By the fall, the movement had grown to about 240 students. We also developed and trained the next level of potential student leaders on how they could lead Bible studies in the dorms. The stage was set! I can remember walking over to the gym where Josh would be speaking. I envisioned 700 people being there the first night, 1,000 to 1,200 being there the second night, and 1,500 people being there the third night. All we needed was for God to raise up another sixty students. We were ready to share our faith, follow up, and had Bible study leaders ready to help them grow in their new walk with Christ. Standing in the gym, dreaming about what God had done to make this happen, all I could do was say, "God, You are so amazing. You are so good. I love you so much."

Then Josh came. I was so excited before the first meeting, I couldn't stand it.

As the meeting was about to begin, I looked around the room and realized that the majority of the people were either students from the different Christian groups, or Christians from the community. Instead of 700 attending, only about 350 people came that first night. The comments on the response cards we collected were all from excited Christians.

The second night of the three-night series, my hopes again were not realized. The 1000-1200 people I envisioned were not there. About 700 people came, but once again, the crowd was predominantly Christian students and Christians from the community. Our encouragements for students to bring their friends didn't seem to be working. I was disappointed, discouraged, but not defeated.

The third night about 1,000 people came instead of the 1,500. Once again, Christians from the community flocked to see Josh. But the non-Christian students, who were our focus, were not there.

After reviewing the comment cards, knowing it was unlikely that sixty new students would have their lives changed by the truth of the Gospel, and that the faith goal of 300 in three years would not be reached, my heart was broken. Silently I said, "God, why didn't You do it? Why didn't You glorify Yourself on this campus as we have prayed? God, why?"

Over the remaining days in November, and the two weeks in December when students were on campus, I avoided talking about reaching the vision of 300 students in three years.

I was devastated, and my faith was shaken. If God wasn't faithful to fulfill what He led us to trust Him for, how could I ever trust Him again for anything? The previous three years, I was motivated daily by this vision that I believed was from Him. I felt I had led astray every student involved in the movement. I didn't know what to do, or what to say. In a way, I became spiritually paralyzed, frozen, afraid to share a word that would encourage students to trust God.

God had done amazing and marvelous things in transforming a ministry of seventeen to thirty-five students, to one of about 250. Lives had been changed for all eternity, students had grown in their love and passion for God. **But**, God didn't fulfill the vision for a movement of 300 in three years. January, February, March... the entire next semester came and went without the 300. Yes, we kept doing many of the good things that had been done previously. At our Wednesday afternoon prayer at 5pm, more than fifty students continued to gather every week. Our weekly meetings continued to have about 150 students every week. But no one was being led from a vision of trusting God for the miraculous.

As I continued to struggle with this reality and prayed, gradually I began to gain better insight into this traumatic crisis of faith.

One of my life verses is John 14:12-14 where Jesus says, "Truly, truly I say to you, he who believes in Me, the works that I do, he will do also; and greater works than these he will do; because I go to the Father. Whatever you ask in My name, that will I do, so that the Father may be glorified in the Son. If you ask Me anything in My name, I will do it."

As I wrestled with this verse in light of what had happened, I began to realize that Jesus said, "Whatever," not "Whenever."

At the age of seventy-five, when God promised Abram that he would become the "Father of many nations," I am sure that he thought, *Wow, this is amazing. I will be a father in nine or ten months.* As the years passed and Sarai didn't become pregnant, they took the issue of the timing of God's fulfillment into their own hands. As a result, Sarai's maid, Hagar, became pregnant and gave birth to Ishmael. Abram wanted Ishmael to become the heir of the promise, but God said, "No, I will give you a son through Sarai."

When Abram was ninety-nine years old, the Lord appeared to him again and said in Genesis 17:1-2, "I am God Almighty; Walk before ME, and be blameless. I will establish My covenant between Me and you, and I will multiply you exceedingly." In verse 5, God continues, "No longer shall your name be called Abram, but your name shall be Abraham; For I have made you the father of a multitude of nations." God also changed the name of Sarai to Sarah, and God fulfilled His original promise to Abraham **twenty-five years** after the initial promise was given.

Later, I was reading through Hebrews chapter 11 which lists the great men of faith and the amazing things God accomplished through them. But I was stopped in my tracks when I read the latter part of chapter 11, vs 36-40

"…and others experienced mockings and scourgings, yes, also chains and imprisonment. They were stoned, they were sawn in two, they were tempted, they were put to death with the sword; they went about in sheepskins, in goatskins, being destitute, afflicted, ill-treated (men of whom the world was not worthy), wandering in deserts and mountains and caves and holes in the ground. And all these, having gained approval through their faith, did not receive what was promised, because God had provided something better for us, so that apart from us they should not be made perfect."

It was primarily through reading, meditating, and praying over the Genesis 17 and the Hebrews 11 passages, that I was able to be released from my three-year time frame... able to move on with a heart of faith and a deeper thanksgiving for all God had allowed us to be a part of in those three years. Unfortunately, it took me almost two years to work through this period of disappointment, grief, and struggle of faith.

During my five years at the University of Delaware, the ministry never did reach the goal of 300 involved students. Despite that, it was an amazing time in which God worked in the lives of students. The ministry grew:

-from the initial twenty-five or thirty students to about 250 being involved in some way
-many, many students became Christians,
-many students grew dramatically in their faith, learned how to share their faith with others, lead Bible studies, and fulfill many other aspects of ministry

As a result of God working in the lives of students through our years in Delaware, at one point I listed thirty-three students who graduated and went on to full-time Christian vocational ministries as pastors, staff with Cru, Young Life, or other missions organizations.

It is interesting to me that years later, I heard that at the University of Delaware, there was a movement of 300 students. Only, it wasn't through the ministry of Cru, but Inter-Varsity.

God did fulfill the vision He had given me, except like the faithful in Hebrews 11, I did not receive what I was trusting God to do, since He chose a different time and a different way.

To God be the Glory for His Amazing Ways.

Chapter 23

FEAR OF FAILURE – WOULD I GET FIRED?

———————∞———————

In addition to this multi-year lesson related to faith, God had another significant lesson for me to learn during my first year at the University of Delaware. Reflecting on my life and motivations, I clearly identified two factors that were affecting me as a person and as a leader. One of those was that I was a "people pleaser," and the other was that I also feared the thought of failing.

The outcome of these two attitudes was that I was willing to work very hard to prevent myself from failing, which also then enabled me to please those around me. Unfortunately, these are not healthy motivations for working hard. I realized that ultimately, my fear would limit me in what I might attempt for God or trust God to do. As a result, I chose to face these weaknesses deliberately and head-on.

To overcome the effects of my people-pleasing tendency and my fear of failure, I concluded that I had to attempt something with two critical criteria: 1) there needed to be a high risk for failure; and 2) it needed to be a high-profile effort whereby if I failed, leadership above me and others around me would recognize it.

As I wrestled with these thoughts, at Cru's National Staff Training in Colorado, the national and area leadership encouraged us to develop a strategy to reach out to student leaders on campus. As soon as I heard that encouragement, I said to myself, *That is it.* From that point on, I began to develop a strategy to reach the leaders at the University of Delaware.

Since it was my first year at the University of Delaware, and only one other staff member on the team had been there the previous year, none of us knew many of the student leaders on campus. The plan that developed was to invite all the student leaders on campus to hear an exceptionally successful businessman speak on "Success in Life." The topic would include both natural factors that enabled success, and defining what true success in life was; namely, fulfilling the purposes for which you were created. The first criterion of high risk for failure was fulfilled since we were reaching out to a segment on campus where no previous relationships or foundation had been laid. The second criterion was fulfilled after I asked Art DeMoss, the founder and CEO of a multi-million dollar insurance company, a good friend of Dr. Bright (founder and then president of Cru), and a member of the Board of Directors for Cru, to be the speaker. When he said he would come and speak, there was no doubt that I was facing my fears head-on.

As a staff team, we worked hard to make the Leadership Seminar a successful event. We chose the best night of the week for students to attend, we sent embossed invitations, the envelopes were hand-addressed to each student, we ordered catered desserts, and, of course, we included a description of Mr. DeMoss' profile, his experience, his accomplishments, and his success. As the night for the Leadership Seminar came, I was both extremely excited, and extremely nervous.

I envisioned and hoped for a room filled with seventy-five to 100 key leaders. The event began at 7:30pm. At 7:15, only about three students not already involved with Cru were present. At 7:20, the limousine of Art DeMoss drove up. As he set aside what he had been reading in the rear of the limousine, he also finished his paper bag dinner.

As we entered the meeting room at 7:25, only about twenty students (including the Cru students) were present. I cringed as I thought of this friend of Dr. Bright giving his time to speak to twenty students. My worst-case scenario for the night was becoming a reality. As Mr. DeMoss spoke, I wondered what he thought about the small number of students who came to the seminar. I wondered if this would be shared with Dr. Bright. Would national or area leadership get a call from Dr. Bright's office and they in turn have a talk with me? If so, what would they say or do? Was there a chance I could get fired?

As the seminar ended, I thanked Mr. DeMoss for taking the time to come and speak. He was very gracious and simply thanked me for the opportunity. As he drove away in his limousine, by faith, the only thing I could say was, "Thank You, Lord, that You knew what would happen tonight, and that You know the plans that You have for my life."

Over the next few days, then the next week, I wondered every day if I would get a phone call from Dr. Bright, national, or area leadership. Interestingly, no one ever called. I never heard a negative comment about my "failure." In fact, via the grapevine, I later heard that our leadership was encouraged that I was willing to take the risk to attempt something significant for God's glory.

After that night, I never feared failure in the same way. Though I have never felt pleased that the attendance was so low that night, to this day, I am thankful for how God used this in my life.

Chapter 24

I Still Do Not Understand Why!

W e received the call from the Northeast Regional Director of Cru in the spring of 1983. He said, "Ron, you have done a great job in trusting God and seeing God raise up a movement of committed students at the University of Delaware. As a result, we would like to ask you to prayerfully consider allowing God to use you to see similar movements raised up in the New York-New Jersey area. The area director role is now open, and we need someone to give guidance to and care for the staff in this area. Will you take a week to seek the Lord, and let us know what you think?"

My initial response was, "Bill, I appreciate the call, and I am willing to pray, but I want you to know that I really don't think I want the job. I have yet to see God do all that I believe He wants to do, and thus, I don't want to raise any false hopes or expectations."

He said, "That's fine, and that is what we would expect to hear from you. But as long as you will go to prayer, that is all we want." I told him I would.

I decided to take a day to be with the Lord. It would be a day where I got away from the house, away from the responsibilities at the U of D, away to pray, read the Word, make a pro-con list regarding staying versus leaving, and pray some more. It amazes me sometimes how the Lord can redirect my thoughts and lead me to another idea, strategy, or direction in such a short period of time. It doesn't always happen that quickly, but by now, I am confident that when God has something in mind, if we seek Him and His will, He is very capable of convincing us of it in a very short period of time.

I started my time with the Lord totally persuaded that I should not leave the U of D. I felt that leaving Delaware before I saw the 300 students involved, regardless of God's time frame, would be a step away from faith and into unbelief. However, as I prayed, my mind seemed to be drawn to open and read Hebrews 11, about the men of faith. As I read through the chapter, and then read Hebrews 11:39, my mind and attention were once again pulled towards these words, "they did not receive what was promised, since God had provided something better for us, that apart from us, they should not be made perfect."

As I sought God's guidance, I found myself asking, "God, for the believers in Hebrews 11, You chose to fulfill Your promise through others. Is that what You want here? Is this what You have chosen for me? Do You want me to accept this new role?" I continued to pray and read through many verses in the Bible, but my mind and spirit kept returning to Hebrews 11. Once again, I lifted up my request for wisdom and guidance. As I again asked God if He wanted us to leave the U of D and take the new role, a calm assurance seemed to answer, "Yes."

Probably twenty questions immediately came to my mind. *But what about the staff team? Who will take over for me? What about Char and the girls? But what about…"* With each "But what about…" a sense of inner calm that God had thought about that and would take care of it seemed to rise up in my heart and spirit.

I went home that evening and said to Grandmom, "Honey, I am completely surprised and a bit shaken. We definitely need to seek the Lord together on this, because today in my time with the Lord,

He seemed to take me to a completely different place. I think He may want us to move to New York. We really need to seek Him together."

Over the next several days, we continued to ask God to guide us and confirm this direction in our hearts, if that was what He wanted. The more we prayed and surrendered our hearts to whatever God wanted, the more we sensed that this was the direction He had for us. After a week of seeking the Lord, I called and told the regional director that I was surprised, but Char and I both felt that God wanted us to take the new role.

Yet, it was hard to think about leaving Delaware. We loved the ministry there. We had great friends and a great church. Char had started a women's neighborhood Bible study through which some women had placed their faith in Christ as their Savior and Lord.

Michelle (Mommy or Aunt Michelle) was going to an excellent elementary school where she was thriving. She had even gathered a number of her friends in the neighborhood to come to our home for a Discovery Group. (By herself at the age of six, Michelle walked down the street, knocked on the front doors of her friends' homes, and ask their parents for permission for them to come to her Discovery Group. Basically, it was a short Bible study on the fruit of the Spirit, using a recording of a song as a starting point.)

Despite all of these positive life realities, we became convinced that God wanted us to take this next step. We put our house up for sale and visited Ithaca, NY, to look for a home. I met with the former New York-New Jersey area director to discuss the ministries, and we began to make arrangements for the move.

Unfortunately, months passed, August arrived and our home had not been sold. Interestingly, neither did the home of the former area director. We could not buy a home without the equity from our home in Delaware, and neither could he buy a house in his new location. As a result, we both realized that if we rented his home over the next year, that might be a good temporary solution to the housing dilemma for both of us.

The downside for us was that it cost twice as much to rent his house as it did for us to pay the mortgage on our home in Delaware. As a result, beginning that August, our housing costs tripled. We would have been able to request an increase in our salary to cover the new costs, but we really didn't have the financial account balance to cover that. Things became very tight financially.

Every day we continued to pray and ask God to sell our home. But the house remained on the market through August, September, October, and November! We were stretched to our absolute limit financially, especially since the heating costs were increasing exponentially due to the cold winter days and nights in Ithaca.

I couldn't understand why God hadn't sold our home. We had sought Him, we had followed and obeyed Him, we had moved away from friends, a wonderful ministry, a great church, we had done all that He had asked, and we had sought to be good stewards of His provisions through all of it. But He didn't seem to be keeping up on His responsibilities as I would have expected. Why?

I think in reality, there will be many times in the lives of each of us when we don't understand why things are the way they are, or why God allows certain things to happen. His ways are not our ways. I again think of Abram. In Genesis 12:1 it says, "Now the LORD said to Abram, 'go forth from your country, and from your relatives and from your father's house, to the land which I will show you...' v. 4 So Abram went forth as the LORD had spoken to him... v. 7 The LORD appeared to Abram and said, 'To your descendants I will give this land...' v. 10 Now there was a famine in the land. So Abram went down to Egypt to sojourn there, for the famine was severe in the land."

Why did God tell Abram to leave his home, lead him down to the land of Canaan, reveal to him that this was the land He had chosen for him and his offspring, and then bring a famine in the land that was so bad, he couldn't stay there, but had to go onto Egypt? The Scriptures never tell us why. All we know is that it happened, and that later Abram returned to live in Canaan.

Finally, in December, our realtor in Delaware found a buyer. We had weathered the financial drought. Why things happened the way they did, I don't understand, except to say we were still learning new ways to walk by faith, trust, and surrender to Him. And we were thankful as we realized that our family was fine, we were making new friends, enjoying a new ministry, going to a new church, and that God had sustained us.

Chapter 25

GOING TO ROMANIA – FEAR
AND ANXIETY – "DON'T GO!"

————————∝————————

G randmom and I were at a national conference with other
campus leadership within the Cru ministry in March of
1985. At one of the meetings, one of our "Heroes of the Faith,"
Bud Hinkson, was speaking. Bud, his wife Shirley, and their two
children had left the United States in the '70s to begin a ministry
behind the Iron Curtain to Russia and the communist countries in
Eastern Europe. Though from time to time we heard stories of what
God was doing, security was very tight so that the lives of those
involved would not be jeopardized.

The primary reason Bud came to these meetings was to ask us
as area directors to prayerfully consider having one of their countries become an area partnership. From the time Grandmom and I
first came on staff, we had sought to go overseas. Initially we were
told we needed more training. After we had sufficient training, we
were told they could not accommodate families in a location where
we thought we would like to serve.

As Bud spoke, he said, "I do not care if you have families. If
you have families, we will do what is necessary for you to go with

your families." After Bud said that, our ears and minds hung on every word he said.

After he was done, Grandmom and I immediately began to talk and pray, "God, would You want this to be something we did as a family, and as a part of Your vision for the New York-New Jersey area?" As we got up the next morning, the two of us discussed it again, and felt that we should take the next step of asking more questions about the specifics of a partnership, and how that would relate to our family. Bud and one of the leaders of one of the countries met with us later that day.

Everything they said caused us to want to pursue the possibility more. We agreed with Bud to continue to pray, and decided to get together again in a couple of days. We would be seeking God in terms of agreeing to a partnership and they would be asking for wisdom in matching us with the right country and opportunity… if we said yes.

We knew this would be a significant and potentially scary step, and thus we prayed, "God, we don't want to do this if this is not within Your plan for us. The worst thing we could do would be to end up behind the Iron Curtain without that being Your desire. So please guide us. Please prevent us from making a mistake." As we continued to pray, God continued to put the need of helping to reach His world on our hearts. A sense of peace and confidence in His faithfulness to guide us settled within.

Two days later, we once again met with Bud. We told him that after much prayer, we felt God was leading us to move ahead. Bud had also been praying, and they wanted our area to have a partnership with Romania. At that point, we knew where Romania was geographically in Eastern Europe, but that was all we knew. Bud shared that the regime of the communist dictator Ceausescu was very oppressive, but the people of Romania were spiritually hungry for the Gospel, and the underground church needed training and encouragement.

As we left the discussion with Bud, we told him we would continue to seek the Lord.

As the following weeks passed, as we prayed, as we read more about Romania, our sense that this was what the Lord wanted grew stronger. It was probably in May or June that we made a final decision to move ahead with the New York-New Jersey area/Romania partnership.

That summer I began to cast a vision for the partnership with our campus directors, and before the end of August had informed all of the Cru staff in our area. We planned to cast the full vision for a summer mission project at our area-wide student fall retreat in October. I cannot remember the text I used as a basis for the challenge I gave to all the students at the retreat, but I do know I told them something like:

> *What I am about to share is not for all of you. If you look at the armed forces, you will notice that the Marines are looking for a few good men. That is what we are looking for this summer. If you are not ready to camp most of the summer in a country behind the Iron Curtain, if you are not willing to face the potential of being interrogated, if you are not willing to live a life of faith and dependence on the Lord, and to share the Gospel where the government doesn't like it, then this is not for you. But, if you are willing to go before the Lord and say, 'Lord I am committed to following You, I am willing to live a life of faith and dependence upon You in difficult circumstances,' and you feel that the Lord is saying, 'YES', this is for you, I need to know that over the next couple of months.*

I will be passing out commitment cards after our meeting. We would like you to take one and pray about this tonight and in the days to come. If, after seeking the Lord, you feel that you are **one** *of the* **few He has chosen,** *then drop your info in the box tomorrow morning, or before you leave after lunch. Or if you decide later, you can let us know through the staff on your campus.*

Of the 300 or so students at the retreat, we received cards back from around ninety indicating an interest. We knew that over the months ahead, a good number would drop out due to the need to take classes over the summer, parental objections, or a variety of other reasons. We hoped thirty-five students would feel led by the Lord to go with us.

As the months passed, we became more excited about what God was doing in preparing our team, but we also became more concerned about the trip for two reasons. To lead the project, and go as a family, we needed to raise thousands of extra dollars of financial support. God had always been faithful to provide as we followed Him in faith, but the thousands of additional dollars we needed did seem insurmountable, at least from our human perspective. The only place we could land with that concern was, if God had called us to lead our area in this partnership, and to lead the team this summer, then He would raise the money in spite of the obstacles. We simply had to live a life of faith and trust Him.

The second obstacle was even more emotional for us. In the spring of 1986, the nuclear power plant in Chernobyl, Ukraine, had a meltdown. We were informed that radioactive fallout had spread over eastern Romania and the Black Sea. During the summer, our teams of four to eight staff and students would be camping at different locations throughout the country for a week to ten days at a time, and then move to another location, so they should be fine. But our family was going to spend the entire six and a half weeks at an apartment on the Black Sea. We were informed that the radioactive fallout would affect the food-fruits,vegetables and milk (cows eat grass!) in the Eastern part of the country and it would have been retained in the sand by the Black Sea. This was exactly where we would be taking our three daughters: Michelle was eleven, Jen was nine, and Kristi would have turned six that May.

Part of the difficulty in making a decision was due to the conflicting reports about the severity of the radioactive fallout. Russia and Romania declared, "All is safe in Romania." But we knew that it wasn't necessarily wise to believe the information coming out of the communist countries. Western predictions differed since Romania wouldn't let anyone from a non-communist country do any testing of the sand or food. Thus from the West, we heard everything from, "It will be fine," to "It would be foolish," to "I would never think about taking my family there." Grandmom and I prayed and prayed for wisdom. Probably only a parent could understand the depth of concern in those prayers!

As a mom, Grandmom experienced a significant degree of turmoil as she considered going, for multiple reasons. Here is what she shares:

Grandmom...

For many months, it seemed as though God had confirmed that we were to go to Romania for the summer and lead the teams. It was a severely oppressed communist country and would, as a result, present us all with challenges, concerns, and fears we had never before encountered. But we became increasingly excited and assured that this was the path God had for us. We asked all those simple questions that seem so important at first. *Where will we live? What shots will we need? Do they speak any English? Do we do everything through translators? Should we take any food? What is the food like? Can we drink the water?* There were lots and **lots** of questions! We had never been outside the U.S. before, except in parts of Canada near the border. This was all new to us! And overwhelming! Once all those questions were out of the way, our minds and hearts were ready to absorb more significant information needed for leading the trip.

To make it even more emotionally challenging, there was terrorist activity in Vienna, Austria, at two separate airline offices in April, not long before we were scheduled to leave. We were flying into Vienna! It was a bit scary to think about. Then there was the nuclear reactor plant mishap (Chernobyl disaster in the Ukraine, April of that year) that would affect Romania and particularly the area near the Black Sea where we would be most of the time. Both were serious events and not to be taken lightly. They certainly caused us to think and pray... again and again. *Should we really be in Romania for the summer with the three girls? Is it wise? Will it be safe?* Fear is a tremendous weapon that our enemy, Satan, can use against a family! We were struggling to determine if God would really have us go. It helps to get as many facts as you can before letting those fears get a stronghold, and we found that it was so important to seek the counsel and prayer support of others who love Jesus. Calls from Cru staff in Europe at these crisis points were tremendously helpful, uplifting, and helped with our perspective.

My concerns and fears were focused mainly on the "safety factors". What loving parent wouldn't be concerned with issues of communism and safety, dangerous radiation potentially in the sand, soil, the food products we all would be exposed to, and the ruthless surprise attacks by terrorists? The "knowns" as well as the "unknowns" were daunting and taunting. After spending much time in prayer and reading God's truths in the Bible, my heart and mind were able to rest in this: It is better and safer to be where God wants you to be, than even to be at home, in those all-too-familiar circumstances that give us a false sense of safety and security. And it was clear once again that He did want us to go to Romania!

There was only one other moment – and it was brief, though it was pretty intense, when I was ready to grab our bags, snatch up the family and go home! Funny how some memories are so, so clear, after years and years. Usually that is because they are connected with so much emotion. And so it was. There we were, standing in the breakfast line at the briefing conference, shortly before loading the buses and heading to the airport in New York City. We were almost at "the point of no return" as far as going to Romania. Suddenly, and without any warning, fear overwhelmed me! I was pretty much paralyzed with fear. Petrified, my stomach and mind were swarming with butterflies! I had to talk myself into staying in line because all I wanted to do was grab everything, the girls and Ron, and bolt out of there! What kept blasting relentlessly through my mind and messing with my emotions was how utterly ridiculous, crazy, and stupid it was to be going to Romania under the present circumstances. *What are we thinking?* That was when I had to quickly, purposefully and continually choose to give all those fears and thoughts to God…over and over and over again. There is a verse in the Bible that says we need to take every thought captive and make it obedient to Christ (2 Corinthians 10:5). That was what I needed to do. I had to choose to give God the flood of anxiety and fear I was experiencing and set my thoughts on what I knew to be true of God: Cast all my anxieties on Him, because He cares for us. God is faithful. God loves us. God is with us. He is our refuge and strength. He has called us to go to Romania. It is better, it is safer to be where He has called us to go, than to be at home! Soon, the overwhelming need to flee was replaced with His peace.

We were going to Romania. All five of us!

Granddad...

Thus, after weeks and months of prayer, wrestling in our hearts, minds, and souls, we stepped out in faith, concluding that the Lord was saying, "I have called you to go and your children are under My care."

By faith in **His faithfulness**, we took the step into the unknown, having no idea all of the **crazy** things God had ahead of us.

Chapter 26

ROMANIA, HERE WE COME

———————◦<————————

At a briefing conference a few days before we went to Europe, all the staff and students going on summer projects throughout Eastern Europe and Russia gathered at the former Kings College in Briarcliff, NY, just north of New York City. At this conference of over 300 staff and students, confirmation of the country to which each student was going became known. In all our recruiting, students knew we were going behind the Iron Curtain, but they had no idea where. We had a total of thirty-seven staff and students going with our family of five to Romania. We established team leaders and divided the other thirty-seven staff and students into seven teams with four to six people on each team. Our family was considered to be the eighth team of the project.The rest of the time at this conference, we focused on getting to know one another and team-building preparations.

Then, we were off to Vienna, where a more country-specific briefing occurred. In Vienna, we developed a project-long plan of where each team would go to camp and meet college students who were on holiday, or what we call vacation. Each team could only stay at any location for seven to ten days. If they stayed longer, it was virtually ensured that they would be called in by the police, or the *Securitatae* (the Romanian equivalent to the KGB or, in the

U.S., the FBI). I had a master sheet that showed where all the teams would be at any point in time. Each team leader was only given the sequence of travel for his team. My role was to oversee and stay in touch with all the teams. I would meet many of the teams as they came to camping areas on the Black Sea, while they would spend a few days in Bucharest, the capital of Romania, or were camping in another location within a three-hour train ride from Constanta`.

One critical aspect of this briefing was the training on how to answer questions if interrogated. We were told we should not lie, yet we could say things to keep from revealing who we were as an organization, and our purpose of seeking to share the Gospel with university students who could speak English. We would not deny that we were Christians. If asked if we were there to propagate Christianity, we would simply say that if anyone talks about his life, usually his religion comes up, and every Christian in that type of situation shares what he or she believes. If asked if we were missionaries, we would say something like, "I simply look at myself as any normal Christian would."

In some situations, if asked a question that would be too revealing, we encouraged them to have a response that didn't answer the question directly. Similar to how Jesus might be asked one question, and He would shift the subject or focus. When the Pharisees brought the woman caught in adultery to Jesus in John. 8:5-7, we read, "Now in the Law, Moses commanded us to stone such women; what then do you say? They were saying this, testing Him, so that they might have grounds for accusing Him. But Jesus stooped down and with his finger wrote on the ground. But when they persisted in asking Him, He straightened up, and said to them, 'He who is without sin among you, let him be the first to throw a stone at her.'" He never directly answered their question. Rather, Jesus redirected the question with His answer. Thus, if they asked if we were here as part of an organization, we might simply say, "While at college, I heard that students could travel to Eastern Europe, it sounded exciting, so I decided to come with some friends." Thus, we were trained to avoid answering the actual question.

During one afternoon of meetings before we left Vienna, several students were individually asked to leave the session. Each was taken to a room with a table and a chair, told to sit down, and informed that someone would be there in a few minutes. The door behind them would suddenly open and lights in the room would go out except for a light directly above the table. Three men dressed in Russian Army uniforms entered the room and barked interrogation questions at the student. Shocked and completely surprised, each student attempted to respond to the accusing questions. Needless to say, it was intimidating and totally unexpected. As the students individually returned to their seats for the rest of the meeting, they were not permitted to say anything. Most just sat there with a look of fear on their faces. After the meeting was over, they were allowed to share what happened, how scared they were, how they couldn't think straight, how unprepared they were for the situation. To say the least, there was a buzz that spread through all the students going to Romania.

This exercise was not intended to be a game. It was **serious**! We fully expected individuals from one or two of the teams to be pulled in for questioning. Later that evening, the training on how to answer questions was repeated. Though the students had listened the first time, the urgency to hear and digest every word was now taken to heart by every student and staff, including your Grandmom and me.

It was after the mock interrogation, the second training on how to answer questions, and the information on what to expect at the Romanian border that the stage was set for the level of fear I had as we prepared to smuggle the movie projector, the three large movie reels, and the other translated materials into Romania!

At this point, you may enjoy re-reading **Chapter 1: Filled with Fear**. The first chapter shares about the trip from Vienna and the fear I experienced as we crossed the border into Romania. If what occurred during the border crossing isn't crystal clear in your mind and emotions, I'd encourage you read that chapter again. This will help you to pick up on what occurs next.

At the end of Chapter 1, I said, "Little did we know that in less than twenty-four hours from the border crossing, circumstances would evolve where the potential for interrogation, detainment, or prison, far exceeded what we experienced at the border." The next chapter shares about those next twenty-four hours.

Chapter 27

"Oh God, Is There Another Way Out of Here?"

————————⟨✕⟩————————

W̲e traveled along the two-lane highway east toward the city of Cluj, Romania. We were told to continue to a particular kilometer marker, pull to the side of the road, and wait. No one ever knew how long it would take to get through the border, so every hour, our contact person planned to check to see if we were there. Thus, we stopped at the kilometer marker and waited.

Finally, a car drove up behind us and stopped. I was told to memorize a phrase in Romanian, to which our contact would respond with certain words. He was then supposed to pull from his pocket a cassette tape and seek to hand it to me, to which I had an exact response. We were then to greet each other with the Christian greeting, *"Pace,"* which means peace. I was relieved to find out that the first car that stopped had Liviu, our contact, in it. Along the side of the road, he took the movie projector, the *JESUS* film and the other books and materials. In exchange, he gave me the *Alege Viata* (a Romanian version of the Four Spiritual Laws), the Romanian-English follow-up materials, and nearly 70,000 lei, the Romanian currency.

In Romania during the reign of Ceausescu, many believers and especially pastors were being persecuted. If people were coming to faith, the communists felt this was a threat to their authority. As a result, effective pastors often experienced one of three outcomes: they could go to prison, they could have their children taken away from them and placed in a state-run orphanage, or sometimes they were given the choice of leaving the country. If they left Romania, they were not permitted to take anything with them. For the pastors who chose to depart, prior to leaving they would sell all of their possessions. The lei they received would then be deposited into a bank account that Christians throughout Romania had established. The lei would be withdrawn and given to missionary groups like ours that traveled into the country and needed the Romanian currency. We would pay American dollars for the lei, which would then be passed on to the pastors who had been exiled to the West.

In 1986, the common "worker" would earn 6,000-7000 lei per year. I was given about 70,000 lei (a lot of money). The reason for this amount of money was that it needed to cover all the expenses for the 37 project participants and our family of five for almost seven weeks. Every weekend, our teams would spend one to two days in a hotel where they could get a hot shower and sleep in a bed. The rest of the time, they slept on a half-inch cushion on the ground in tents, had cold showers, and got food from the *piata* (a market in the town) or ate at restaurants.

One of my initial responsibilities as we drove across Romania was to meet different teams in different cities at predetermined locations at specific times. We always had at least a plan A, B, and C. Generally, that meant we had a designated time each day at the specific location, meeting on the hour, or half hour, three hours in a row. An example was meeting by the statue in the town square on Tuesday at 1pm, 2pm, or 3pm. If one of us wasn't there, we would have the same plan for Wednesday, and if Wednesday didn't work, Thursday. If neither of those meeting opportunities worked, there was a general emergency alternative plan for meeting several days later in another city.

After the transfer of materials with Liviu, he took us to his flat/apartment. He warned us not to speak any English as we walked from our parked car to the flat, to walk twenty feet behind him, and not to walk too slowly. We had a wonderful meal with Liviu and his wife, and we were off to continue on our journey.

While in Vienna, we had purchased hotel "coupons" from the official Romanian Travel Agency. We were permitted to stay at government-selected hotels, which had designated floors for foreigners, with assigned tables in the restaurant. We were warned by our European Cru staff that we should expect the rooms where we slept and the tables where we ate to be bugged. In other words, whatever we would say, we were to assume it could be heard by someone connected to the *securitatae*. At the travel agency, we purchased the exact number of adult coupons for Grandmom and me, and the exact number of children (reduced cost) coupons for each of the girls to last the number of days we would be in Romania.

As we arrived at the designated hotel that first night, I went to the reception desk, filled out the form, and put the appropriate number of adult and children coupons on the desk. The attendant picked up the adult coupons but said, "No children coupons, just adult." I responded that the Romanian travel agency said they were supposed to also accept the children coupons. The attendant then raised her voice and said, "No children coupons, you must pay with adult coupons!"

I knew if I gave her our adult coupons, we wouldn't have enough for the rest of the summer, and we would have too many children coupons. Thus in the best way I could, I said, "We purchased these coupons at the official Romanian travel agency, and they said—"

With that, the attendant began yelling at me, "I told you no *copii* (children coupons). I said *nu*, and that means *nu* (no)! You will meet the manager tomorrow."

I stood there shocked, speechless, and now scared once again.

I didn't want to cause a problem whereby the authorities would be notified, so I responded by offering to pay American dollars.

The attendant barked back at me, "No, you will see the manager tomorrow. Go!" I picked up the coupons, the keys, and silently began to pray, "Oh God, don't let this turn into a mess tomorrow morning."

Grandmom, Michelle, Jen, Kristi, and I all walked up to our rooms. We had told the girls that they were not to say anything about the project teams or our ministry while we were in the hotel or restaurants. Throughout our time in Romania, they all did extremely well at this.

The next morning, I immediately went to the reception desk and explained the situation to the manager. He was very agreeable, and he took the *copii* coupons. I walked away from the desk saying, "God, thank You for not allowing this situation to cause problems, and that the authorities didn't come. In Jesus' name. Amen."

I returned to our hotel room. The suitcases were just about packed so I decided to carry a couple suitcases down and put them in the car as we went to the restaurant for breakfast. As Char and the girls headed into the restaurant, I headed for our car. Looking down the parking lot, I saw three policemen going through the trunk of a car in the lot. Immediately, I thought, *Oh man, if they go through our trunk and find the evangelistic booklets, the follow-up materials, and 70,000 lei without a receipt from an official Romanian bank, we are really in trouble.* Why would an American who had been in the country for one day and was staying in the country for seven weeks have the yearly pay for more than ten people in his possession? Being caught now would have been exponentially worse than having the guard find the Jesus film, etc. at the border. I prayed, "God, please have them leave and not stop us."

I quickly walked to the Volvo, threw in the suitcases and walked back into the restaurant. After sitting down, I said to the three girls. "Girls, you have been so good, but I have a request. Until we leave the hotel, please be extra good and do not cause a problem. Eat as quickly as you can. I will really appreciate it. Thanks." The girls were wonderful.

After breakfast, we organized our luggage so we could carry all the bags out in one trip, and even planned to pile smaller things on laps so we could get out of the parking lot as quickly as possible. As we walked towards the car, I immediately looked towards the end of the parking lot where the police had been. They were standing at the exit for the hotel, waiting for the next car to come their way. I said silently, "Oh God, is there another way out of here? I can't drive down to them." As we continued to walk to the car, I looked down at the other end of the hotel. I couldn't be certain, but there seemed to be a little alley between the hotel and the next building. As I pulled out of our parking spot, I turned left rather than right towards the hotel exit. At the end of the parking lot and the building, I was right, there was a narrow alley. I didn't even know if the Volvo could make it through, but I had to try. Slowly, I pulled into the alley. There were three inches of clearance on each side of the car, at most. Tight, worried, but determined, we drove through without hitting either side. As we reached the road, I turned right to continue away from the hotel and headed out of town. Silently I prayed, "Oh God, please don't let them jump in their car, catch up to us, and pull us over." Ten minutes later, I took a deep breath and said, "God, thank You again for protecting us."

Over the next couple of days we traveled across Romania and met at the designated meeting points, only experiencing a couple one-hour meeting delays. The teams had come into Romania by train, all being questioned by the border guards, but with no serious interrogations. Day by day, we grew in confidence and thankfulness.

After several days, we arrived at the motel/apartment/restaurant complex that had been arranged for us. It was about 8pm, we had been driving all day, and all of us were exhausted. As soon as I got out of the car and began to walk to the reception area, a man walked up to me and in perfectly clear, no accent English said, "Do you want to change money?" Changing money like this was against official Romanian law, and was referred to as being done on the black market. Yet, it was pretty common since anyone could get a much better rate of exchange in currency than could be received from a Romanian bank. The practice was often overlooked by Romanian officers, but it was also something that the *Securitatae* or police could hold over you if you were caught doing it. As a result, no one involved in the summer mission was permitted to exchange money this way. Thus, I told the man, "No thank you." We later found out that this man, whom the girls gave the nickname "Mr. Cool," was the highest-ranking *Securitatae* leader in Mamaia, the peninsula on the Black Sea where we were staying. He was also the only Romanian I ever heard speak English without a strong foreign accent. Throughout our weeks at this apartment/hotel/restaurant complex, I heard him speak several other languages as he sat outside the restaurant and had conversations with people.

As was the case at the other officially approved hotels, we had an assigned table to eat at in the restaurant. Every lunch and dinner, a band played the same eight songs over, and over, and over again. As the band would take breaks, Freddy, the young sixteen-year-old lead singer, would often come to our table to practice his English. He was the one who told us there were five *Securitatae* agents watching us. Four of these men made themselves **very** obvious to us. One was positioned on or near the beach, one would always walk in between the buildings and follow Char and the girls as they walked to the bread store every morning, one was the head

Securitate man, and one man was always inside the restaurant. We were never able to identify the fifth man, but he could have been stationed inside one of the buildings and watched the front door of our flat.

As part of the housing arrangements, a meal plan for breakfast, lunch, and dinner was included at the restaurant. Every time we walked into the restaurant, the inside agent would be somewhere in the restaurant talking to other Romanians. As soon as we sat down at our assigned seating, he would walk over and sit down at a table about five feet from us, listening to every word we said at every meal.

This environment set the stage for two unique situations that occurred during the summer. These stories, I will tell next.

Chapter 28

"How Did They Know I was at the Campsite?"

———————⋈———————

As I mentioned earlier, one of my responsibilities during the summer was to meet with each of the teams as they traveled to different campgrounds across Romania, meeting university students, and sharing the Good News as they went. There were several campsite locations along the coast of the Black Sea. One of the sites was just north of where we were staying in Mamaia. On one particular afternoon, Char and I met with the leaders of a team camping at that location. We met in the center of the beach where no one could hear what we were saying. We talked through what the team had been experiencing, what their next steps would be, and some other details. However, as a result of that conversation, it was important for me to get down to their campsite to give them something that night.

I waited until it was dusk before I left. We even unscrewed the light bulb outside our door to lessen the possibility of being noticed leaving. Pulling out of the parking lot, I headed south for a couple of miles, made a U-turn and then headed north towards the campsite. This was done to help ensure I wasn't being followed. By the time I arrived, it was dark. That afternoon, the team leaders had told me exactly where their tent was pitched. I parked my car and walked directly to their tent. I was there for only a couple of minutes, went back to my car, and again drove south of where we were staying for a couple of miles, made a U-turn to head for our complex and turned into the parking lot. It seemed that all had gone well and no one had seen me.

The next morning as we walked into the restaurant, before we were ten feet inside the door, Freddy, the lead singer of the band walked directly towards me and said, "I heard you were at the campsite last night. What were you doing there?"

Shocked and surprised, I thought for a second and said, "Oh, we met some Americans on the beach yesterday, and I just took something to them."

Freddy said, "Oh," and walked away.

Prior to that morning, Freddy had never been in the restaurant till the noon meal. Emotionally, I was shaken.

As we went to our assigned table, I couldn't believe they knew I was at the campsite the night before. I wanted to talk about it with Grandmom as we sat down, but unfortunately, "Mr. Ears," the agent at the table five feet away, had taken his position.

Knowing that somehow they knew where I had driven that night made me more uneasy when, a week later, a two-tone Dacia with a Bucharest license plate parked in our lot. In the country of Romania at that time, 99 percent of the people with cars drove Dacias, the only Romanian-built car. They came in one of four colors: white, blue, yellow, and cream. However, for the first time ever, we saw a two-tone brown and cream-colored Dacia, with two antennas sticking up from the roof. Curious, one day I walked by and looked into the car. Inside, in clear sight, was a car telephone, something rarely seen even in the U.S.

Why would this car be in our parking lot a week after I had been at the campsite? Of greater concern was the fact that within days, your Grandmom and I were scheduled to leave for six days to do a training camp for the underground church.

Chapter 29

THE LA DODGERS

———————◇———————

As planned, a team of four arrived with reservations to stay at the complex where we were for three weeks. The first week they spent time with us as a family, getting to know our three daughters. The second week they would take care of the girls while Grandmom and I went to a city about three-and-a-half hours away on a special mission for the underground church. The third week, the four-person team would unwind, and do ministry meeting students nearby.

We had been asked to spend five days providing training in evangelism and training on how to walk in the power and guidance of the Holy Spirit to the underground church. The underground church was referred to as The LA Dodgers within our ministry. This stood for "**The L**ord's **A**rmy," which was "**D**odging" the authorities. The Lord's Army consisted of a group of very committed evangelical Christians who were ministering within the context of the Orthodox Romanian Church. If anyone's commitment to this organized movement became known, it was certain they would either go to prison or have other severe consequences.

However, these believers were hungry for teaching from the Word, and for training in how they could more effectively share the gospel. They had secretly approached our ministry and asked for training to take place throughout the country. We were challenged to have the privilege of leading one of the five-day training sessions.

The week before we left for the training, we went into Constanta, the nearby city, to buy Romanian clothes and shoes. The owners of the shoe store were very upset with us that we would want Romanian shoes. Everyone except for the communist officials in Romania was relatively poor. There weren't a lot of extra shoes to be had. For us as Americans to buy the shoes that the Romanians wore was only seen as an opportunity to deprive the people of the few resources they had, or as a means to mock them. But for us, as we went to provide the training for the underground church, we wanted to melt into the crowd as much as possible. Our shoes as well as our eyes were two of the most obvious giveaways that we were from the West. Westerners could always be identified by the quality of the shoes they wore. Unfortunately, we couldn't find any shoes in our size. With regard to our eyes, we were told by Romanians that they could tell we were from the West because they could see "life" in our eyes. Most Romanians would never look directly at those walking by them. Thus, our plan was to look down when we walked along the city street.

As we prepared to leave for the training and as I daily saw the two-tone Dacia from Bucharest, I continually pondered, *Why was that car parked in our parking lot? Did the authorities somehow know what we were going to do? Would they question our girls while we were away?* Grandmom and I deliberately chose not to tell the girls where we were going or what we would be doing. We simply said we were going away for a vacation, a "holiday" to celebrate our anniversary.

The special two-toned Dacia left the parking lot every morning around 8:30am, and returned around 5pm. The morning we left for the training, the Dacia pulled out as anticipated.

The plan was for two of the members of the other team to watch the girls while two of them drove with us to the city of the training.

They would then immediately drive the car back to Mamaia. There was one intersection everyone had to go through to leave the peninsula of Mamaia, and just prior to that junction, the roads turned into four-lane highways, two lanes going in every direction: north, south, east, and west. We were heading south, and needed to turn right and head west to leave the peninsula. As I pulled up in the right-hand lane, I looked around for the unique Dacia. I was the second or third car back from the red light at the intersection. On the inside lane of the cars that were pulling up going west, for one second, I thought I saw the brown and cream car. However, my view was obstructed by the cars to my left. The light changed and we had to move. As I made the turn west, I was still unable to determine if that Dacia was the one from Bucharest, but I knew where it was in the line of cars behind us. As we traveled west towards the countryside, one by one I saw the cars in front of the questionable Dacia turn, but it remained about 300 yards behind us. I could clearly see it, but I could not tell its color or the markings from that distance. On we traveled for about twenty minutes, and for twenty minutes, the car continued with us.

Finally, I thought, *I have got to find out if that is the car from Bucharest.* I slowed down and pulled to the side of the road where there was an empty bus stop. As I came to a halt, I looked in my rearview mirror. The car was gone. I turned around and could see dust flying up on a dirt farm road. Just as we had slowed down and pulled off the road, the car had turned off the main road.

We continued to travel west another twenty minutes to where we needed to turn right to head north. I pulled into a gas station on the left side of the road, turned around, and waited to see if the brown-cream Dacia appeared. We waited for about fifteen minutes, but the car did not appear. Thus, we decided to continue north towards the city where the training would occur. Just before we arrived in Galati, we switched into clothes that looked more Romanian.

The two team members riding with us dropped Grandmom and me off at the assigned location, and then returned to Mamaia. As we waited on the sidewalk in front of a movie theatre, we chose not to look into the eyes of those who walked by us, while keeping our heads looking down.

Finally, a man approached us, asking the right two to three questions, and then showed us a cassette tape. We had found our contact. We followed him, walking about ten feet behind him to the flat where we would meet others.

Each night before the sessions, people began arriving by twos or threes around 5:30pm, at ten-to-fifteen-minute intervals. We would usually arrive around 6:45pm. We taught from the Scriptures and provided training from 7pm until about 9pm. Two Romanian translators were there with us. This was followed by about a half hour of prayer. Then we would be ushered out. Over the next one-and-one-half hours, those who came would leave the apartment by twos or threes, again about every ten to fifteen minutes. The training occurred during the last week of July and it was **very** hot. But to prevent anyone from hearing or seeing what was taking place, all the windows and internal shutters were closed. About forty people packed themselves into the small room, sitting on chairs, and every available spot on the floor or standing with backs pressed against the walls. Due to the heat from the summer day, the absence of air conditioning, the closed windows, and closed shutters, the room was hot when we began, and hotter still when we ended. But every believer there listened intently to every word we spoke through our translators.

I know it was our intent to go and minister to the needs of the underground church, and I am sure God used us in their lives. But what I know more fully is how God used these humble, godly people in our lives. We have never seen people more hungry for God's Word. Nor have we ever met people more broken and humble before the Lord. Though we could not understand all their words, we will never forget seeing these men and women get on their knees, and passionately pray for God to be worshipped, glorified, and for Him to use them in the lives of others (despite the potential outcome of imprisonment). They pleaded with God for these things with groaning and tears. Their hearts, emotions, and their entire beings were poured out to God. We didn't understand all the Romanian words being spoken, but they were unforgettable times of prayer as we heard, felt, and understood the **heart** behind the spoken words.

A second thing that we will never forget about these Romanian believers was their sacrificial, giving spirit. Through the translators, we found out everyone had been saving their money together for the previous month, so they would be able to buy chickens and feed us. As were ushered to the table to eat, they eagerly watched us!

In the process, we also found out about culturally appropriate eating manners, especially in light of the scarcity of food. As we were served soup the first night, as is customary in the U.S., we emptied the bowl. We were then graciously served a second bowl of soup. However, as we ate, we observed that our translator did not empty his first bowl, and of course was not served a second bowl. In fact, he left half of his soup in the bowl, which was then taken from the table. Later, we asked him about what we observed. Our translator told us it was customary to leave soup in the bowl. By doing this, the soup could be poured back into the pot and served another day. Food was scarce and hard to obtain for the average family. We felt horrible that we had eaten so much, and were sure to stop eating and leave our bowls with food in them the rest of the week.

However, the people themselves would have never mentioned this to us, only our translator.

Though we were supposedly the honored guests for this week, we were the ones who became humbled and felt honored to be in their presence. Even today as I picture in my mind this special week, I see them on their knees, pleading with God to use them for His glory.

However, while we were away, back at our apartment complex, the authorities apparently were a little frantic about our sudden departure. We heard later that each of our girls had been taken aside separately and were asked by the *securitatae* where their parents were. Fortunately, they didn't know and could only legitimately answer that we were on vacation for our anniversary.

Chapter 30

THE MISSING JELLIES –
A CHILD'S FAITH

———————∝———————

It was a beautiful day on the beach at the Black Sea. Jen had taken off her jellies near the water's edge to go into the water. When she returned to pick them up, they were gone. The tide was rising and a wave had whisked them away. She immediately saw one of them and swooped it up. The other one could not be seen… anywhere. It had quickly disappeared in the murky, roiled waters.

You may be wondering, *What are jellies?*

In the spring of 1986, before we went to Romania, the rage in girls' shoes were jellies. They were basically a slipper-type shoe made of soft rubber that came in different clear pastel colors like pink, blue and green. The girls each had one pair for the summer.

One fact we were told about the radioactive fallout from the Chernobyl atomic power plant disaster was that the sand at the sea would absorb and retain the radioactive material longer than other surfaces. We were concerned about the effect this might have on the girls if they continuously walked on the sand. Thus, we bought each of them jellies, and told them they had to wear them on the beach at all times, except when they went into the water. It definitely made us all look a bit different on the beach, but sometimes a parent has to do what a parent has to do.

When Jen's jelly disappeared in the waves, she immediately called out that she had lost her jelly! Back and forth we went with our hands in the waves, seeking to at least *feel* the jelly. Our eyes scanned the surface, trying to catch the slightest glimpse of color. Nothing! After several minutes, Grandmom and I were ready to give up, when Jen said, "Jesus can see where it is. Let's ask Him to help us find it."

Grandmom and I looked at each other with doubtful hearts. What should we do? We didn't want Jen to be disappointed if it wasn't found, thinking it might somehow diminish her trust in God! At the same time, we didn't want to tell her *not* to pray. Thus, we decided to hold hands and pray something like, "Jesus, we know You are alive, and You can see all things from heaven. We know You can see Jen's jelly right now, and we ask You to help us find it. Thank You that we can come to You with everything. We pray this in Your name, Jesus. Amen."

Immediately after praying, Jen stuck her hand back into a wave to see if she could feel her jelly. Excitedly she yelled out, "I've got it, I've got it. Jesus found my jelly!" In that instant, it landed right in her stretched out hand!

Grandmom and I looked at each other, somewhat ashamed of our unbelief. Oh what parents can learn from their children, those with **the faith of a child!**

Chapter 31

"You Did What?"

———————⚭———————

Almost every morning at about 10am, Grandmom would walk with Michelle, Jen, and Kristi to the bread store. They would walk from our apartment out to the main road, or they would walk along the edge of the beach, for about one-fourth of a mile south to a *piata* (outdoor market), which also had a bread store. The bread in Romania had no preservatives, so after a day, the bread would be dry.

As they did this every morning, they could see one of the *Securitate* men following them as he wove his way in and out of the various buildings towards the *piata*. He was there every day, without fail.

As the weeks went by, Grandmom increasingly became annoyed that this man would follow them every day. There is also a degree of stress that comes with being constantly watched. Relief from this stress gets played out in different ways for different people. This is one of those ways...

A few days before we left the Black Sea, Grandmom decided to pull a trick on the stalker. As with every other day, guess who was walking along with them to and from the *piata*? Only he was on a path just off the beach...always there, always following. At one point, Grandmom glanced around, trying to give the man the impression that she was checking to see if someone was following her, while not looking right at him. She was purposefully trying to look suspicious!

Once Grandmom was sure they were in his sight and not hidden by an occasional building blocking his view, she stopped and appeared to pull something out of her bag. Again, she looked over first one shoulder, then the other, in a suspicious way, to see if someone was looking. She caught a quick glimpse of the agent hidden behind a bush, watching them. Grandmom then walked up to a trash can on the beach and appeared to carefully place something inside the trash can. As she pulled up her hand, she again looked around, giving the appearance that she was hoping to do this without being watched.

She then continued with the girls along the beach towards the *piata* to buy our daily bread. After a few minutes, before turning to leave the sandy beach, she looked back toward the trash can. Sure enough, the agent was bending over, pawing through the trash to see what she might have secretly sought to hide. Grandmom simply laughed and smiled with satisfaction.

When they returned from their jaunt to get bread, one of the girls was quick to exclaim, "Guess what Mom did?"

Hearing what she did, my response was, "You did **what**?"

Chapter 32

THE FEMALE ROMANIAN
BORDER GUARD

———————◇———————

The day before we left Mamaia, we were working hard to clean and pack. In the afternoon, something that does not occur in the U.S. happened once again. Due to a lack of water and power shortages, the authorities would often shut off the water supply. Since we were trying to clean and scrub things down, not having water was an undesired hindrance.

To know when the water was turned on again, either your Grandmom or I left the water line open in the kitchen. Despite the lack of water, we worked hard and were able to get things done so we could leave the next morning. Exhausted, we went to sleep immediately.

In the middle of the night, Grandmom was "wrestling" in her sleep. She wasn't fully asleep, nor was she fully awake. She was dreaming about a waterfall pouring down over the side of a mountain. As she continued to dream, she also gradually became slightly more awake.

Suddenly, she awoke thinking that she heard water flowing. She got up, and splash! Both feet landed in a puddle of water. She woke me saying, "Ron, get up, we have a flood."

I jumped up out of bed. In the kitchen, water was pouring over the lip of the sink. Grandmom turned off the water, but what a mess we had! Water was close to one inch deep on the uneven floor throughout the kitchen, hallway, living area, and into the bedrooms. The area rugs were soaked, as was some of what we had packed.

Immediately, we got buckets and towels and began mopping up the water. Bucket, after bucket, after bucket of water was soaked up from 3:30am on towards dawn. But what were we to do about the soaking wet rugs that had begun to bleed their red dye on the floor? We picked them up and after sopping out as much water as we could, we hung them over the railing outside, using our hands to push even more water out of the rugs. Then we got cleanser and tried removing the red dye from the floor. We made progress, but were without a perfect outcome.

Around 5am, we went back to bed to try to get an hour of sleep before we got up to bring in what we hoped would be slightly drier rugs. We had planned to depart by 7am for our trip across Romania. The rugs were no longer dripping, but they were far from dry. We really felt bad that we had to leave with the rugs still wet. But the good news was, the floors were really clean! We packed the car and departed on time, not knowing if we had done a good enough job cleaning everything up, or if at some point in the future, we would receive a bill for the restoration of the floor or rugs.

We traveled across Romania all day, and stayed in a hotel that night before approaching the Romanian–Hungarian border.

The next day was a sunny and warm Romanian summer morning. As we headed towards the border, Grandmom and I discussed the issues related to crossing the border. Though it was difficult getting into Romania, we had heard at times it was just as tough getting out. Why this would be the case, we didn't know. We could not imagine what someone would want to smuggle out of Romania in those days. This time, I wasn't filled with fear, for we weren't carrying anything we thought would present a problem.

Still, the cars stretched for a half mile as drivers waited for the somewhat meaningless search. Finally, our turn came. Again I tried to get a line with a male guard and was surprised when a woman came out of a building and approached us. My guess is she had come off a break, and to say the least, was ready for action!

She went through all the suitcases, piece of clothing by piece of clothing. When she opened the trunk, she immediately seized upon a guitar we were carrying back for one of our team members. The team member had brought it with her for the summer. The Romanian guard began saying that it was a Romanian guitar and she was going to take it.

I immediately objected, and said, "This is not a Romanian guitar! Look inside and see the maker." She escalated the volume of the conversation trying to intimidate me, but as she did, fortunately a male officer approached who was obviously her superior. I appealed to him regarding the guitar. He barked a few words in Romanian at her, and she returned the instrument without another word.

Then she proceeded to go through everything in the trunk. She found Grandmom's personal Bible and the journal she had been keeping through the summer. She took both of them inside the small guard station, and we heard her in an angry tone yelling *Baptista*, the term they used for most non-Romanian Orthodox, evangelical Christians. At this point, Grandmom and I became concerned.

Throughout the summer, Grandmom had written down a lot of what had happened in a way that only she could truly interpret. I guess you could say it was written in code. She never used Christian words, and she left blanks where people's names could be added once we were out of the country. Apparently, these empty spaces were of particular concern to the guard. The arguing inside went on for about five minutes, back and forth between the female guard and her supervisor.

Finally, she came out steaming. She handed us the journal and Bible and in a gruff way informed us we should leave. As she stomped away, we packed up as quickly as possible and passed through the border to the Hungarian side. We received only a couple questions from the Hungarian border guard, and we were on our way.

We drove for about twenty minutes into Hungary before stopping along the road for a picnic lunch. Our Romanian friends had graciously packed us a lunch of chicken and corn on the cob. As I sat there and relaxed for a moment, suddenly I felt what seemed to be a huge, heavy weight lift from my mind and body. It was totally unexpected and felt kind of weird. I had not been aware of its reality, but it was apparent that the constant watching eyes of the five *Securitatae*, and the challenge of overseeing the teams had taken its toll on me emotionally. During the summer:

-two teams were interrogated extensively by the police/ *Securitatae*

-one team had all their money, passports, and materials stolen from their tent. Fortunately, the passports were recovered, while emergency arrangements had to be made to provide them with money for the rest of the summer

-one girl had all her clothes stolen from her tent

-one team had been chased by three, ten or eleven-year-old gypsy boys with machetes

-numerous other events and minor emergencies occurred.

Yet the resounding reality through everything that occurred was **God had been faithful to guide, lead,** and **protect** in every circumstance. More importantly, hundreds of college and high school students had heard the Good News for the first time in their lives. The challenges, experiences, and learning opportunities of the

Summer Project of 1986 in Romania were completed. Our lives had been changed forever.

However, that is not the end of the story for our family and Romania. There are a few more stories from other years to share...

Chapter 33

Three More Tales from Romania

For the next four years, I oversaw the summer projects and vision trips to Romania. Following the Summer Project of 1986, due to the intensive and extensive observational efforts of the *Securitatae*, it was determined that it might not be best for our family to stay in one location again for the majority of a summer project. Thus, as we went again as a family in 1988, we stayed most of the time in the capital city of Bucharest, while also traveling to other cities to meet with teams camping throughout the country.

While in Bucharest and the other locations, we never felt the "heat" of the *Securitatae*'s efforts. In addition, something that may have reduced the pressure was the official university invitations we began receiving to take professors and guest lecturers to the universities in Bucharest. I guess there is nothing like official sponsorship with positive results to reduce some of the pressures.

Three quick, memorable stories come to mind that I'd like to share:

The Train Debacle of 1988.

Our second summer project was coming to a close. Overall, the teams had done well, except for two tragic incidents it would be best not to relate.

Grandmom and I had just finished a training camp for some believers in Timisoara (the city where the revolution against communism began in December of 1989). As a family, we were ready to leave the country by train to go to Vienna for the project debriefing.

Some of the wonderfully hospitable believers from the training were taking us to the train station. We had purchased tickets for a second class overnight sleeping car, had given all our extra lei to the believers in the city, and thought all would be fine. The train finally arrived in Timisoara about an hour late. As we searched for our train car number, we realized it was quite a distance past the end of the train platform. Thus Grandmom, the girls (now thirteen, eleven, and eight) and I had to walk on rather large jagged rocks past about eight train cars to arrive at our car. It was so far back, the slight bend in the tracks prevented the engineers from seeing where we needed to board the train.

Without a platform, the steps up into the train were about three feet up from the rocks below. Grandmom was helped up by our Romanian friends, and I was able to climb up in the car next to her. As we both arrived in the doorway of the cars, the train jerked and began to take off with Michelle, Jen, and Kristi still on the ground. Immediately we realized it would be impossible to get the girls on the train. Our only option to stay with them was for us to jump off onto the large rocks. I went first, and chose to jump out backwards, knowing that I could fall on my backpack (luggage bag, not book bag) as I hit the rocks. The girls were crying, yelling in fear and reaching up for their Mommy. Romanians on the train were hanging out the windows, trying to get the attention of the conductor, to no avail. It must have been quite a spectacle.

In her concern for her girls, Grandmom turned around to face them as the train was moving away. All she could think about was getting off the train and back to them. Thus she jumped face forward, from the moving train. As her feet hit the rocks, her entire body continued the forward motion downward. Rather than having a backpack provide a buffer and absorb the impact of the fall, the weight of her backpack propelled her body even more forcefully into the rocks.

Her arms, knees, legs, and face bore the damage from the crash. Immediately, our Romanian friends rushed to her side to see if they could help. Initially, she couldn't move. I climbed out of my backpack and rushed over. As the pain from the initial impact subsided, a gradual assessment of her injuries began.

Her face had some minor cuts, but nothing severe. She seemed to be able to move her legs, though not without pain. One arm had been severely smashed against the rocks, and it was questionable as to whether it was broken. Slowly, with the help of the Romanians, she was able to get up. We cautiously moved towards the platform. On the platform we got bottled water and a clean cloth to wash the cut areas. Her right arm continued to be in significant pain. We wrapped it in a makeshift sling, and quickly decided not to take her to a Romanian hospital where the slightest injury could become a major long-term problem due to the lack of sanitary utensils and the poor training of physicians during the communist regime. Since she was able to walk and move, we decided to try to find a way to get a ride to the Romanian-Hungarian border where the train would be delayed due to the searches being done before entering Hungary. No passengers were normally allowed to board at the border, but we were going to try.

With the help of our Romanian friends, a man with a car (there were no official taxis) was hired to take us to the station. The Romanians negotiated the price, and actually paid for it from some of the money we had given them, since we no longer had any lei.

Grateful to them for making the arrangements, the five of us crammed into the little Dacia and drove away. I was very thankful that we were able to travel, and that we would be able to get Grandmom good medical attention within twenty-four hours at a hospital in Vienna. That is, I was thankful until, instead of turning west to go to the Romanian border, the driver turned east. I immediately objected, pointing in the other direction. He motioned to me to calm down, and touched his head to say, "I know, I know." The longer we went east, the more concerned I became. But there was nothing I could do. Finally, he turned into a parking lot and got out of the car.

There we sat, the five of us crammed into a parked Dacia, Grandmom hurt, the driver knowing no English, and us not knowing enough Romanian to communicate clearly in an emergency situation. We sat and sat in the car, not knowing what to do.

All I could do was pray, "God, what is going on? Char is hurt, we have no lei, no way to contact anyone, the driver who has already been paid has disappeared, and I don't know what to do. Lord, the only thing I can do is look to You to help us."

Suddenly, the driver reappeared with a five-gallon can of gas. He poured it into the gas tank, jumped in the car, and we took off — this time in the correct direction.

To my surprise, however, he didn't seem to be in much of a hurry. Other cars heading toward the border went whizzing by us. He seemed quite content to drive along going thirty-five, or forty kilometers an hour. A couple of times I motioned to him with concern on my face and in my voice, while pointing to my watch. He simply grinned, put his hands up to say things were fine. It had now been well over an hour since the train had departed from Timisoara. And unlike us, the train didn't have to stop at a bunch of traffic lights along the way.

Finally we pulled up to the station at the Romanian-Hungarian border. Our train was still sitting there. I immediately said, "Oh

God, thank You that it is still here." We got out our luggage, and the driver helped me by taking Grandmom's backpack up to the building. We found a seat for Grandmom, and I went into the station with my tickets. Unfortunately, no one was sitting at the ticket counter. I looked around and no one seemed to be present to whom I could speak. I walked out on the platform, and saw what appeared to be an officer in the army. I approached him and showed him our tickets. He knew a little English. Seeming to understand our situation, he asked me to wait where we were standing, and he took off.

Ten or fifteen minutes passed. *Where was he? What was happening? How was Grandmom doing?* All these thoughts ran through my mind as I stood where he left me and waited. Finally he returned, and asked where my family was. We went to Grandmom and the girls. Amazingly, he proceeded to apologize for what had happened with the train, and then led us past our assigned train car and compartment. He escorted us up closer to the front of the train, helped Grandmom and the girls get on the train, and took us to a first-class compartment.

There were no questions about how long we had been in Romania, where we had traveled, or why we were in the country. He simply wished us a safe journey and was gone. We sat there in amazement.

Once we crossed the border into Hungary, as a family we prayed something like:

"God, thanks that Mommy (Grandmom) didn't get hurt so badly that we couldn't continue to travel. Thank You for the help of the Romanian believers. Thanks for the man who drove us to the border, and that he was honest enough to get us there even though he had already been paid the money by the Romanian believers. Thanks that our train had not passed through the border before we got there. Thanks for the kind officer. Thanks for this nice first-class compartment. Thanks that Mommy (Grandmom) will be able to get good medical treatment in Vienna. Thanks that we will be able to get to Vienna on time and participate in the debriefing with our teams. In Jesus' name. Amen."

As soon as we arrived in Vienna, Grandmom went to a hospital and got an x-ray of her arm. The report was no broken bones. **Yeah**! It would take a month or more for the deep bruises to heal, but she would be fine.

As we sat in our room that night in the hotel in Vienna, all we could do was give thanks to God for the way that He, in His faithfulness, had worked things out. To God be the thanks and praise.

Gypsies On The Train

It was early in the summer of 1989. I wasn't leading the project that year, but I was in Romania prior to the project's arrival to make arrangements for some of our teams to go to a Black Sea beach resort where hundreds of the university students went during the summer. Three of us were traveling on the train together from Bucharest to Constanta. A Cru campus director in the New York-New Jersey area, a youth pastor for college students from a large Baptist church in Texas, and me. The senior pastor of the Baptist church in Texas was a former Cru staff member, and it was his desire to partner with Cru by sending some of their college ministry students with the summer project.

The youth pastor was a big Texas boy, about 6'4" tall, weighing in at probably 250 pounds. As we traveled together and kind of kidded each other, we gave him the nickname Hoss (we stole the name from the TV show *Bonanza*. Hoss was the big, rather burly brother on the show). Our Hoss had never been out of the U.S. before, and in fact, hadn't traveled much outside of the big state of Texas.

He was a friendly guy, but he felt awkward and didn't know how to respond to things being so different in Romania. The country was still communist, so that was a whole different experience in and of itself.

For the long-distance trips on the passenger trains in Romania, we would often buy second-class tickets, which placed us in a six-passenger compartment. As we boarded our assigned train car, we noticed what appeared to be an entire clan of gypsies also boarding. I would guess that 50 percent of those in our train car were gypsies. As the three of us set our backpacks on the overhead racks and took our seats, a gypsy woman with her two children came in and sat across from us.

The woman was probably around thirty-something, with a daughter about fourteen years old, and a son around eleven years old. Though we exchanged a brief greeting, we immediately knew that little conversation would occur between us due to the language barrier.

Being from Texas and the youth pastor for a large 5,000-member Baptist church, Hoss was up on the latest trends in clothing apparel. Since we were heading towards the beach, Hoss decided to wear his bright fluorescent yellow aqua shoes that he had bought prior to the trip. In the U.S., this was part of the latest summer beach attire that had just come to the stores. The shoes had a slight rubber sole, with the tops made of a nylon material that would dry out very quickly. People could wear them on the beach or wear them into the water. Normally, as we traveled in Romania, we tried to limit the amount of attention that might be drawn towards us by keeping the volume of our voices lower than normal and by wearing clothes that minimized our western look.

But this was Hoss, from Texas. Despite being told about being overly loud and enthusiastic, he continually forgot. When it came to clothes, Hoss wore the most noticeable colors and patterns that could be found. For him, wearing these bright fluorescent yellow aqua shoes was just who he was.

After the train pulled away from the station, it didn't take long for the gypsy girl to be attracted to Hoss's aqua shoes. It was obvious from her constant staring at his feet that she wanted what Hoss had on his feet. As a rule, gypsies often preferred bright colors that would stand out. And Hoss's shoes definitely did that.

After about a half hour, the girl finally motioned towards Hoss, pointing to the shoes, indicating that she liked them. Hoss, in his friendly way, just began talking about them, how much he liked them, and that he had just gotten them before the trip. It was obvious to me that she didn't understand a word he said, but that didn't matter to Hoss. He was just being Texas friendly.

Finally, the girl pointed to the shoes, pointed to him, and then pointed to herself. Hoss didn't know what she was trying to say. Thus she did it a couple more times, with the final time pointing to the shoe, and then pointing to her feet. The gypsy girl wanted to buy Hoss's aqua shoes.

Hoss immediately said no, he wasn't interested in parting with his new aqua shoes. She seemed disappointed, but seemed to accept it. That is, at least for a minute or two.

If there is one thing that is characteristic of the gypsy culture, it is that saying no to them one time when they want to sell you something does not work. They tend to be very forward and very repetitive in their attempts to make a sale. Thus, I was not surprised when after a minute, she asked again, and then again, and then again. Hoss continued to say no in an appropriate way, but gradually, her repeated asking began to get to him. It was a three-hour ride to Constanta.

A pattern seemed to be emerging. The gypsy girl would ask Hoss for them two or three times, be told no, wait for ten to fifteen minutes and then begin to ask again. This went on for an hour! Personally, I was kind of amused at her persistence, and the unique difference that was true of the gypsy culture. However, Hoss began to struggle more and more with her relentless badgering.

Then the shocking word came.

Hoss could take it no longer. As she asked for the aqua shoes one more time, Hoss lashed out, "No, you dummkopf!" There were only a few words that could have clearly communicated anything between us and the gypsies. Unfortunately, this insulting German word meaning "dumb head" or "blockhead" was one of them.

Immediately, it seemed like the air was sucked out of the compartment. The mother, daughter, and brother's eyes shot back an intense glare at Hoss. He had rudely and loudly insulted the girl.

Two things were widely known about the gypsy culture in Romania at that time. First, an insult to one member of the clan would be considered an insult to the entire family. The second thing was that almost every adult male carried a knife, and they did not hesitate to use it.

Shock filled me as the words rang out. *Hoss, what did you say,* I thought.

The young boy stopped his glare and moved out of his seat towards the cabin door to go tell the clan what had been done to his sister. **Fear** filled me. What was going to happen? If the boy told the clan leaders, in thirty seconds we could have ten men with knives at the door.

Then, the mother started laughing, making a joke out of it, and putting her hand up to stop the boy. The tenseness in the compartment immediately vanished. We joined in chuckling, trying to make a joke of it, while also apologizing.

Though Hoss was big, and there were three of us, we would have been defenseless against the knives of the clan. Stories of gypsies stabbing people abounded in the Eastern European countries through which they wandered.

As the train continued to roll along, I silently gave thanks to God that the mother chose to make a joke of what occurred. Fortunately, another request for the aqua shoes never happened.

Crushed at the Stage

It was my first time in Romania after the overthrow of Ceaucescu and the communist government. As the two Cru campus directors from the New York-New Jersey area and I walked down the streets of Bucharest, I couldn't believe the difference in the people. As people walked along the sidewalk, their heads were no longer tilted downward. Children seemed to play more freely and loudly in the park. Bright colors seemed to emerge from the *piatas*. Despite the bullet indentations and marks on the walls from the revolution, there was a new sense of life in the air instead of the grayness of life that had existed for decades in Romania.

New freedoms were being experienced by the people and the culture. Through contacts with professors at the University of Bucharest, we had been invited to give lectures related to the historicity and reliability of Christianity, and other apologetic topics. It was exciting to be part of the dramatic changes taking place.

One afternoon, the two directors and I gave an optional class lecture to a packed auditorium of around 400 university students. We were encouraged by the enthusiasm of the students, and the earnest and intelligent questions being asked.

At the end of our talk, we told everyone in the room we had brought with us a couple of books we would give to anyone who wanted them. One of the books, *More than a Carpenter,* by Josh McDowell had already been translated into Romanian, while the other book was written in English. As I began to close the session, John and Doug, the two campus directors, pulled out the boxes of books and placed them at the front of the raised stage where we had been sitting.

As I made my final comment about the free books, I jumped down and asked them to come down to the front to get them. Immediately, the auditorium erupted with movement. Like a stampede of cattle, the students ran to the front of the room to get the books.

The three of us were shocked. John and I immediately realized that we better get off the floor. We jumped up the three feet to the stage. Unfortunately, Doug didn't respond quickly enough. He was pinned against the stage as the students pushed in to get the books.

Within minutes over 400 books were distributed, and it was good for Doug that they went that fast. Bruised from being crushed against the stage, Doug vowed he would never again give away books in Romania without protective padding!

The first NY-NJ Area Romanian Summer Project Team in 1986

Michelle 11, Jen 9, Kristi 6, and Ron with a completed puzzle in
Romania. 1986

A familiar sight as we drove across Romania in 1986. A farmer and hay wagon on the road.

Ron meeting with a key pastor and the Cru National Director of Romania on the beach in Mamaia

Meeting with the team Ron visited later that night at the campsite and was questioned about it the next morning

Char with our translators and a host family at the training for The Lord's Army-the Romanian underground church

Secret training and teaching for the underground church, in the apartment of believers

Gathering at the beach towards the end of the 1986 Romanian Summer Project

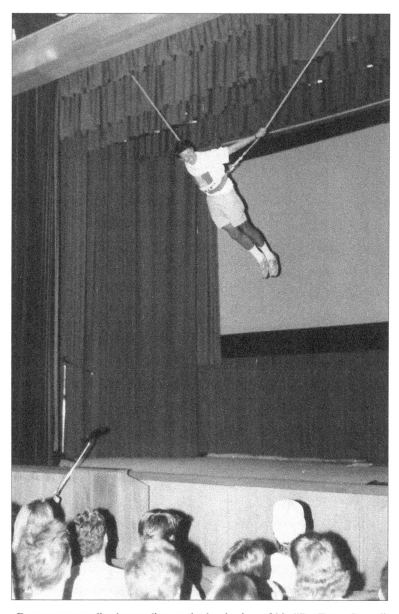

Ron unexpectedly descending at the beginning of his "Re-Entry Stress" talk at the 1986 Debriefing in Vienna

The Bystrom family ready for the 1988 Summer Project to Romania

Char and the girls on the train traveling from Vienna to Romania in 1988.

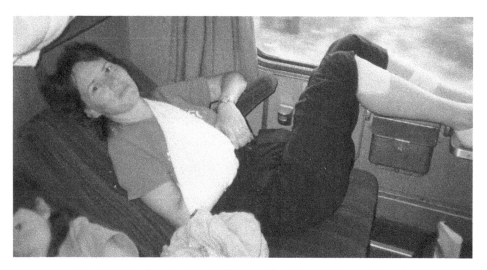

Char in the train returning to Vienna after the accident at the train
station in Romania.

Chapter 34

A FAILURE IN EVERY WAY – THE MOST DIFFICULT DAYS OF MY LIFE

———————⋈———————

F or five years I had given oversight to the university ministries of Cru in the New York-New Jersey area. Although there were many aspects to the job I liked including: casting a greater vision for believing God to a greater number of staff and students; guiding, counseling and developing the campus directors and the Cru staff throughout the area; and the opportunity to speak at numerous university campuses, I deeply missed an ongoing relationship with students into whom I could pour my life.

Thus, when challenged to consider a new experimental position where I would continue as an area director but also return to the role of a campus director, I was very excited. Since the present ministry director at Princeton University was intending to leave staff and get a job in Washington, D.C., the regional director saw Princeton as a viable campus location.

The thought of ministering to the Princeton students, recognizing how God had blessed and gifted them, excited me. Knowing that the university was established by a Presbyterian synod, that the crest still stated *"Under God's Power May She Flourish,"* and aware of the impact of former university presidents like John

Witherspoon and Jonathan Edwards, or students like Robert Speers (Student Volunteer Movement), caused me to hope that future graduates would go on to glorify God in remarkable ways.

In February of 1987, we traveled to Princeton to give Grandmom a sense of what it would be like for us to live there.

I can clearly remember that first trip to Princeton. Things did not start out very well.

An hour after we jumped into the car, it began to snow. In fact, what ensued was one of the worst storms of the year. A trip that would normally take four hours took nearly seven hours. Rather than arriving in the early afternoon with a rather easy drive, we arrived exhausted around dinner time. After eating, we began to look for a motel. Since it was just your Grandmom and me on this journey, I unfortunately returned to my old ways of taking a road trip. That meant reservations to stay at a particular hotel had not been made. Once the severity of the storm hit, everyone traveling that day abandoned the roads and headed either for home or a hotel room.

Hotel to motel to motel we searched, trying to find a room. After more than an hour of searching, stopping, and asking at motels for a room (no cell phones, smart phones, or GPS back in those days), we finally found a motel with an open room. As we fell on our bed completely wiped out, though thankful for a warm room and a bed, it was obvious that things had not gone as we would have wanted or expected in the first hours of this venture to Princeton. Yet, hope reigned and we looked forward to what God had for us in the days ahead.

Plow trucks had done their job by the next morning and we were able to meet the present director and his wife, visit the university, and gain some more information about the campus. I had been to Princeton University in the fall, but that was my only previous visit. Though Princeton University existed geographically in the New York-New Jersey area prior to this year, the Ivy League

Schools had been an "area ministry" unto themselves. Now, for the first time in five years, Princeton was under my jurisdiction.

The more I thought about the opportunity the more excited I became. Yet, I also knew that Grandmom and the girls would have preferred to stay in Ithaca. God had enabled us to build a new home outside of Ithaca where we had great views and could see herds of deer run on undeveloped land. If we looked out our front picture window at just the right angle, we could gaze upon Cayuga Lake in the distance. We had great neighbors, a good church, a good staff team that assisted me with area responsibilities, and everything seemed fine...except for me.

Grandmom could sense better than I could myself that something within me wasn't right. Though she was happy and would have preferred to stay in Ithaca, she was willing to sacrifice the relationships she had, the beautiful setting in which we lived, the joy she got from being one-and-a-half hours from her mom, dad, and the farm she grew up on, so that I/we could fulfill the ministry to which God seemed to be calling me/us. The sacrifice that Grandmom was willing to make for God and me spoke profoundly to my heart in terms of her love for me and desire to follow God.

Finally, towards the end of March, a national decision was made to try the experiment of the area director-campus director role. There were four of us in the country who chose to test out this new role. I couldn't wait for it to happen.

This decision, however, meant we needed to sell our home and move to New Jersey. During the four years we had lived in the new house we had built, the cost of real estate had jumped dramatically in Ithaca. It was a sellers' market. We thought about selling the house without a real estate agent since someone had already expressed an interest in buying it. The real estate woman who had helped us obtain the land and led us to a trustworthy builder heard through the grapevine that we might be moving. She gave us a call and asked, if she could bring us a buyer, would we be willing to sell the house through her? We agreed. Two days later our house was sold for twice the price we paid for the land and the construction of our house.

I felt that God was giving us immediate confirmation in our transition to the role and the move, and I said something like, "God, You are so good. You know me and how You designed me to serve You best. You brought this new role into existence just when I needed it. You have sold our home without any effort on our part. Thank You so much."

Within the next couple of weeks, Char and I arranged to make another trip to New Jersey to investigate the real estate market. We knew things were much more expensive there than Ithaca, but with the money we had made through selling our home, we felt we should do fine. We soon found out how wrong we were with that assumption.

Seeking to gain more information about the housing market in Princeton, we walked into one of the real estate agencies in Princeton (during this period of time, no one had personal computers, and there was no Internet to do research on our own). We sat down with a real estate agent and she began asking us questions to help her know how we might qualify for a home. We told her we had three daughters and needed a room for an office in the home. Thus we were looking for a four-bedroom home. We told her what our salary was and she kind of grimaced. We told her the amount we could put down for the purchase and she actually chuckled and said, "You don't really expect to buy a home in the Princeton do you?"

We were shocked at her apparent rudeness. It was our first step towards understanding exactly how expensive it was to live in the area. Through the present Princeton University Cru campus director, we were given the name of a Christian real estate lady and began the actual search for a home through her. We quickly found out that if we went outside of Princeton to West Windsor, the town just east of Princeton, the cost for a similar home would drop $50,000. We also found out that if we lived in Plainsboro, the town just north of West Windsor, the same home would drop another $50,000. We were encouraged to find out that The West Windsor-Plainsboro School District, like the Princeton School District was one of the best in the state.

We knew the students at Princeton University were very time-conscious. Through discussions we learned that if we told students it would take fifteen minutes to travel somewhere, they would automatically jump to the potential loss of time being thirty minutes. Thus, if we lived fifteen or more minutes away from the Princeton campus, in the students' minds, they would lose an hour's time simply by traveling to and from our home. Losing that hour would prohibit many students from coming to our home. We thus decided that the best case scenario would be to live ten to twelve minutes away.

During our first real estate trip, things were rather discouraging since there weren't a lot of houses on the market in our price range, and the few rental homes we saw were in terrible condition. But it was still early, and who knew what the Lord might do?

As I reflected on the price of homes and our needs, I realized it would be easier to get a home if we found some co-owners who would help us. The idea was to approach some of our ministry partners with an investment opportunity. If I could find three investors who could provide $10,000, $10,000, and $5,000 to increase our down payment by $25,000, that would get us where we needed to be.

I brainstormed all the possible friends and ministry partners who I thought might be able to help. I sent a letter challenging them to prayerfully consider helping us while making a good investment at the same time. Unfortunately, everyone said they wouldn't be able to help.

Though a little disappointed, I wasn't discouraged at all. I felt we still had a lot of time. Someone could change his or her mind, and/or God could help me come up with another idea.

Another possibility was that God could simply raise the additional financial support we needed. I realized that to move down to New Jersey, even if we rented a home, it would cost nearly twice what we were paying for housing in Ithaca. It also seemed that everything from food to clothing was more expensive. The girls were also getting older and as a result, school activities would also increase our financial need. I determined that even if we did buy a home, we would **not** want to pay more for it on a monthly basis than we would spend if we rented a home. As I did the math, I realized we needed to see God raise about $2,000 of monthly support to move and cover our growing family needs. That was a lot of money, but God was able, right?

As the weeks passed, I worked hard to find new ministry partners in New York. Unfortunately, we gained no new partners from my efforts. I then traveled down to south Jersey. FarFar and Nana were away at their little home in Ocean City, from Memorial Day through the month of June. Thus I had time to work on gaining ministry partners in south Jersey without interruption. I looked through all our key partners and identified those who would most likely be able to refer us to their friends.

Unfortunately, though I wrote them letters and tried to be in touch with them through the phone, I had little success in actually talking to them. Then things got worse. By the end of the first two weeks in June, I not only hadn't seen any new ministry partners join us, but several friends let us know they could no longer be active in our ministry through financial contributions. We lost about $200 in monthly donations! Things were not going in the right direction.

I continued over the next two weeks to re-contact people who might be able to help us. The responses I heard included that they couldn't help at all, couldn't help at this time, or I was asked to get back to them in a few weeks. I began to experience a serious emotional crisis. For three months — all of April, May, and June — it seemed everything I did went sideways or backwards. By the first week of July, a summary of our situation was as follows:

1) We did not have enough money to buy a home at the same cost as renting a home without receiving $25,000 from other investors.

2) I did not know anyone else I could ask to make an investment to help us buy a home.

3) In late May and early June, Grandmom made two trips down to New Jersey to see homes. We had looked at all the listed rental homes and nothing seemed to fit our needs. Even if we paid twice as much per month as we paid for our home in Ithaca, the rental homes we saw had holes in the walls, kitchen floors with missing tiles, odors, or other problems. We found a nice home in Plainsboro to possibly buy, but we couldn't afford it without investors. After the last trip down to see homes for sale or rent, Grandmom left in tears because we found nothing that would work.

4) In the previous months, despite significant attempts, I was unable to raise a single dollar of the additional $2,000/month we needed for housing, clothes, food, school activities, etc.

5) Instead of gaining additional ministry partners and financial support, we had lost $200 of monthly commitments over the previous months, which increased our need to $2200. I had been in contact with all of our present ministry partners and none of them could increase their giving, and I had no new referrals to contact.

6) We needed to leave in a couple of weeks to attend our national staff training in Colorado. We would arrive home from this training on August 1st. On August 2nd, we needed

to begin packing everything we had so we could move out of our home by the closing on August 7.

7) I called our real estate agent in early July, and there were no more homes on the market to rent.

8) We had nowhere to go and live. No home to buy. No home to rent.
   I had led our family to a place of destitution.

After attending a church service the first Sunday in July, I returned to FarFar's and Nana's condominium in south Jersey. **As I closed the door, the reality of these facts and my selfishness hit me. I am going to be very honest and tell you exactly what was going on in my head and my emotions.**

At that moment, I was overwhelmed by the thought/reality that I was a complete failure in every aspect of my life !

1) I was a **failure** as a husband — I had followed my own selfish path to job fulfillment – removing my wife from relationships, family, and home

2) I was a **failure** as a father — My girls didn't want to leave their home and friends in Ithaca. No, only one person wanted that, **Me.** Plus, now I didn't even have a place for my girls to lay their heads.

3) I would be a **failure** as an area director – If we didn't have sufficient financial backing, I wouldn't be able to fulfill the job I had been doing the previous five years.

4) I would be a **failure** as the Princeton University Cru Campus Director – I had a new staff team arriving at the end of August. Due to our lack of funds, they wouldn't have a director either.

5) All my vain plans and creative ideas for investors, for getting potential ministry partner referrals, for raising additional contributions from previous partners had failed. And

more significantly, I had **no one** left to **call** about any of our needs.

What had I done? My spirit became totally broken.

I fell to the floor and all I could do was cry and pray, "Oh God, what have I done? What have I done? God, there is nothing more I can do. My family is going to be homeless. We have nowhere to live. I have no one to turn to. I have failed in **every way**. Oh, God. What have I done?"

How long I cried, I do not know. Definitely an hour or more. I was a totally broken man.

But at some point, the goodness and grace of God began to enter. In the midst of my tears, words of the hymn "*It is Well with My Soul*" by Horatio Spafford began to break through to my mind. "*When peace like a river attendeth my way, When sorrow like sea billows roll, Whatever my loss, Thou hast taught me to say, it is well, it is well with my soul.*" Over the next half hour, in the midst of my continued tears, the words of the hymn flowed in and out of my consciousness, until I found myself singing "*it is well, it is well, it is well, it is well with my soul.*"

As God's grace continued to move within me, I then found myself singing the hymn *Great is Thy Faithfulness* by T.O. Chisholm. Slowly, I began to remember how God had done the miraculous for us in the past. A quietness and peace began to settle within me.

Unable to cry anymore, I got up from the floor. I had no idea what would happen in the days to come, but I went to sleep that Sunday night with peace.

On Monday morning around 9am, I received a phone call from a past friend named George. Grandmom and I had met George and his wife through a Sunday school class when we lived in Delaware. He and his wife were not close friends. We had never been to their home, nor had they ever been to our home. Our only contact was through the Sunday school class at church. We had never sent them our ministry newsletters, and hadn't talked to them at all for over six years.

As George began the conversation, initially I had a little difficulty remembering who he was. He said that in the previous week, he had been talking to Wayne, another friend from that Sunday school class who had supported us and kept up with our ministry. Apparently in conversation, Wayne casually mentioned our ministry transition, our associated needs, and in particular, our need for investors.

On the phone, George related to me that from the moment he heard about us, he hadn't been able to get us off his mind. He said that one of his parents had recently gone to be with the Lord, and that they had committed to tithe from the inheritance they received. He and his wife had been wrestling with how God wanted them to allocate this money. Until he talked to Wayne, he had no idea. George said, "We now believe we know what God wants us to do. We want to give you $10,000 towards your need for a home. No strings attached. I know that I will not be able to rest until I commit that money to you."

I sat there with the phone in my hand, stunned, speechless, hardly able to respond. "Thank you" was probably all I could manage to say, but it had to have been filled with such unbelievable gratitude and emotion. **What an amazing answer to prayer**! Plus, here was a couple that had surrendered their all, in a sense, to God and had ears to hear from Him. **What an amazing example!**

We talked about arrangements that would have to be made to receive the money, and I said I would review Cru policy. We caught up on each other's lives, prayed on the phone, and hung up. I sat there astounded and just said, "Thank You, Lord!"

A few moments later, my phone rang again. A businessman named John was on the phone. Back in early May, John had been one of the first men with whom I attempted to get an appointment and had asked for possible ministry partner referrals. John owned his own business and from comments he had previously made to me, it seemed that he was well connected with a number of other businessmen in the area. During the remaining weeks in May, and through June, I made follow-up calls almost weekly. He never responded. As July came, I decided to stop contacting him.

On the phone John said, "Over the last week, I haven't been able to get you off my mind. I have the names of six businessmen that I will personally be in touch with about your ministry. I would like you to give them a call later this week. I am sorry it has taken me so long to get back to you, but here it is."

That Monday night, I had a conversation with another person I had known for a long time. After sharing some of what God had done earlier in the day, he said, "I'd like to loan you the other $15,000 that you need. Don't worry about paying it back until sometime in the future when you sell the home."

I was blown away. In less than thirty hours from my over-whelming despair and brokenness, God had miraculously provided.

I called Grandmom and told her all that had happened in the last thirty hours. On the phone, we cried in amazement and thanked God for **His amazing faithfulness**. I said to her, "Honey, we need to figure out a way for you to get down here to see some houses before we leave next week for staff training."

She said, "I don't know how I can do that, I wasn't planning on coming to New Jersey and there is so much to do before we leave."

I said, "Okay, let's just pray about it and think things through. We don't have to make a decision tonight. In fact, I need to be in touch with Edith (our real estate agent) and talk things through before anything else can happen. But let's be praying. Okay?" Grandmom agreed.

Tuesday morning, I called Edith. We talked through the homes that we had seen previously, and discussed which ones were still on the market. She also mentioned some new listings.

By Thursday of that week, Grandmom said she thought if she worked hard, she and the girls would be able to drive down to south Jersey on Monday. Fortunately, since it was now after July 4th, FarFar and Nana had returned from the shore and said they would be able to take care of the girls as Char and I went up to West Windsor/Plainsboro to look for homes. All day Tuesday we visited houses. The house we had seen and liked the most in Plainsboro in May was still on the market. In fact on Tuesday, we went to see the house two times. The house had the four bedrooms we wanted and we really liked the open layout of the house. Immediately we envisioned the house filled with college students.

Both Grandmom and I felt this was the house for us, but we wanted to pray about it overnight. On Wednesday morning, with peace in our hearts, we called Edith and put in an offer for the house. With her help, we also began to contact banks to obtain the best mortgage we could find. Wednesday night, the people got back to us with a counter offer. After more prayer, we countered their offer. By Thursday morning, we got word that they agreed. Grandmom and I drove up from south Jersey on Thursday afternoon to meet with bank officials and sign the necessary paperwork. Everything was being rushed along since we had to leave by 7am on Friday morning to travel out to Colorado for our staff training.

At 10pm on Thursday night, we walked out of the real estate office. All the negotiations and the documents required to purchase the home had been completed and signed. A closing date was set for the first week in September, but the owners agreed to allow something very unusual. They said we could move all our furniture into one large room and the garage of their house prior to settlement since we had nowhere else to put it (storage units weren't as prevalent back then as they are today).

As Grandmom and I got in the car at 10pm, before I started the engine, we paused to spend a few moments thanking, praising, and worshipping our faithful Father.

Around 7am Friday morning, we departed with our three girls on the 1,700-mile, three-day trip to our Cru training in Fort Collins, CO.

To this day, I think that Sunday afternoon and night at my parents' condominium was the most difficult day in my life. Never before had I felt like such a miserable, selfish failure. Only one other day came close to how hopeless I felt. That was the day I received the paycheck for $275 in our account when we lived in Oklahoma and Grandmom was pregnant. But the hopelessness and inner emotional pain of that day in New Jersey reached deeper into my soul than I knew was possible. Never before had despair penetrated so far into my being. And yet...

God showed up. In my most broken, helpless, and needy hour, God put the words of a song in my heart. Words that said, *"It is well with my soul"* and then followed it with, *"Great is Thy faithfulness."* He lifted me up spiritually and emotionally. Then the next morning, He began to unfold the work that He had done in people's hearts over the previous weeks, to pour out **His amazing miracle** of **provision** and **care**.

As the school year began at Princeton University, we moved into our new home. Enough ministry partners had been gained in the remaining weeks of August so I could do ministry while continuing to work on raising funds.

By God's **grace**, I didn't fail as a husband. I didn't fail as a father. I didn't fail as an area director. And I didn't fail as a campus director. Once again, I was learning more deeply to trust God in the midst of difficult circumstances, and to abide in what I already knew to be true of Him. **Oh Lord, my God, great is Thy faithfulness!**

Chapter 35

GOD GUIDES IN A SPECIAL WAY

———————⌀———————

A s I walked to our cabin, **I knew I had to seek the Lord with all my heart.**

Grandmom and I were at the annual Princeton University Ski Safari. It was a week of skiing, sledding, Bible teaching, and relationship-building between students and the Cru staff involved in the ministry at Princeton. The Safari occurred during the last week of January, between the first and second semester at Princeton University. I was going to give the main message the next night, but was completely unsettled about what I should actually share.

As a ministry, we were excited about the growth in the number of students involved in the ministry. At our first ski safari in 1988, there were probably ten students. Around eighty students were at this Ski Safari, which was encouraging. The students were growing in their love and commitment to one another, and their desire to see Christ glorified on campus. Yet for most of the students, there seemed to be an underlying disconnect in terms of a total surrender to God. While desiring to live for God, it appeared that the expectations of parents, extended family, professors, or their own plans might supersede God's desired direction for their lives.

God envisioned leading the nation of Israel, whom He had delivered from Pharaoh and Egypt, into the Promised Land. Yet due to the influence of the ten spies, the people failed to embrace God's promises and His desire for their lives. As a result, everyone over twenty years of age, except for Caleb and Joshua, failed to experience what God had promised could be true for them. They failed to enter and experience that land flowing with milk and honey.

The next night, I would be speaking to eighty very gifted and blessed university students. Students whom I believed God wanted to use in extraordinary ways. Yet I feared that just as the the words of the ten spies caused the Israelites to miss God's best, failing to enter the Promised Land, these students, due to the many voices speaking into their minds, could miss the eternal impact that He had created them to fulfill.

As the snow squeaked beneath my feet, these contemplations filled my mind. I knew once again, I needed the Lord to show up and guide me.

Entering the cabin, I got out my Bible, placed it on the bed, and then got on my knees to pray. I prayed something like, "God, I really do not know what to do, what to say, how I can encourage these students to seek first Your Kingdom, Your righteousness, Your purposes. There are so many voices constantly speaking into their minds that may or may not be from You. God, I only want to say what will draw them to You, to acknowledge that **You** and no one else is **Lord** in their lives. Oh God, You know what You want for each of their lives, how You designed them, how You gifted them, the purposes You have for them in view of the eternity ahead. God, **please** guide my mind and thoughts. I desperately need You. In Jesus' name. Amen."

As I ended praying, immediately thoughts related to **The Princeton Pledge**, a commitment used by the leaders of the Student Volunteer Movement at the turn of the 20th century, came to mind. This was a pledge of total surrender to God. In fact, beyond that, it was a commitment made by university students to follow God to be missionaries for the rest of their lives, if God so led. Just before departing for the Ski Safari, in somewhat of a haphazard way, I had thrown a few books into my backpack. One of those books was written by John Mott, a leader of the Student Volunteer Movement. In it, the pledge that they used was stated.

I knew the worldview and life orientation of today's student was unlike that of a student in the early 1900s. Most students today expected to graduate, go to grad school, or take their first job for a year or two, and then transition to another role or job. The notion of being hired by one company and staying with that firm till retirement was long gone. Thus, the idea of making a commitment for life as a missionary would not relate or connect. I spent the next hour or more looking at Scripture and thinking through how I could communicate the heart commitment of total surrender to the Lord, yet present it in a way they could embrace.

I am sorry to say that I cannot recall the introductory biblical text I used the next night when I spoke. But I can remember placing a seventy-five-foot rope across the room where we met! Around the rope, about one-quarter of the way down the seventy-five feet, I wrapped some half-inch black electrical tape. I explained that the length of the rope reflected time. Eternity past was seen extending on their left side of the tape. Eternity future was to the right side of the tape. The one-half inch of electrical tape represented an individual's lifetime. I asked them to look at that piece of tape, noting how small it was in comparison to eternity past and the eternity yet to come. As it says in the book of James, "You are just a vapor that appears for a little while and then vanishes away." (James 4:14b)

I asked them, "For whom and for what are you going to give and live your life? Think of those who are encouraging you regarding your future focus and purpose in life: Your professors, parents, friends, the companies that want you to give your life to advance their goals, or the focus of their ambitions. Worldly wisdom seeks recognition, wealth, influence, and power now. Unfortunately, this is **sooooooooo** short-sighted. Let me ask you, if you live for these things and even if you attain great fame, who will remember it in 10,000 years? (I pointed to the rope about eight feet down from where the tape could be seen to illustrate where 10,000 years might fall) If you became the President of the United States, will that be remembered in 10,000 or 20,000 years? If you live for the purposes of this world, they will vanish into oblivion in the life ahead?

But, what do the scriptures say will happen if you seek first His Kingdom and His righteousness?

First, all the needs you have in this life will be provided by your Heavenly Father. Matthew 6:33

Second, you will recognize, as it says in Ephesians 2:10, "For we are His workmanship, created in Christ Jesus for good works, which God prepared beforehand so that we would walk in them." You will fulfill the special roles and purposes for which God uniquely designed you. There is only one person on earth, and actually, there will only be one person in all eternity with your exact DNA. You are uniquely made to be who you are: to fulfill the purposes which God has prepared for you, that you should walk in them. That is an astounding reality to consider.

One of the verses that both humbles me and blows me away is what Jesus said in His high priestly prayer in John 17:4. There He says to the Father, "I glorified You on the earth, having accomplished the work which You have given Me to do. Now, Father, glorify Me together with Yourself, with the glory which I had with You before the world was."

In this verse, Jesus is reflecting on His life, with both eternity past, and eternity future in view. But what does He say regarding His earthly life?

He amazingly says, 'I glorified You, having accomplished the work that You gave me to do.' God the Father had a specific role, plan, and purpose for Jesus to fulfill. As the Father had those purposes in mind for the Son, He similarly has uniquely and wonderfully made purposes for each of you. In John 20:21, Jesus said, "…Peace be with you; as the Father has sent me, I also send you."

In 1 Corinthians 3:11-15 it says, "For no man can lay a foundation other than the one which is laid, which is Jesus Christ. Now if any man builds on the foundation with gold, silver, precious stones, wood, hay, straw, each man's work will become evident; for the day will show it because it is to be revealed with fire, and the fire itself will test the quality of each man's work. If any man's work which he has built on it remains, he will receive a reward. If any man's work is burned up, he will suffer loss; but he himself will be saved, yet so as through fire."

This passage is written to Christians. It is a challenge concerning how each person built, lived, and what he or she accomplished in this earthly life. I believe the gold, silver, and precious stones are the things that a Christian uses when he or she fulfills the purposes that God has for them in this life. I believe that the wood, hay, and straw are the things that represent the works that fulfilled the voices of those who were not seeking first God's kingdom and purposes, but rather the accolades and glories of this world.

The question is, *whose* voice *and whose purposes will you follow in your life?*

Will you live for the things of this world, or will you surrender totally to the God who:

-is a lot smarter than you
-created you uniquely and wonderfully (DNA like no one else)
-had eternity past and eternity future in mind when He prepared the good works that you have the potential to fulfill,
-will love you, lead you, bless you, and enable you to glorify Him now and forever?

As many of you may know, it was through something called The Princeton Pledge that Robert Speers of Princeton and John Mott of Cornell used to challenge the college students of their day to a commitment to serve the Lord. That commitment was to give the rest of their lives to serve as missionaries to help to fulfill God's Great Commission.

Last night I wrote up a revised Princeton Pledge. It is not a commitment to be a missionary for the rest of your lives. But it is a serious commitment that recognizes His lordship, and your willingness to change directions in your life, if He so leads. I would like you to take time to pray over this commitment tonight. I do not want a quick or an emotionally-driven response. I want a total heart, mind, soul, and spirit response.

The commitment card says this:

The Princeton Pledge (revised)

In view of the fact that:
   -God created me uniquely and wonderfully for His purposes, which He prepared for me before I was born (Psalm 139:1-18; Ephesians 2:10),
   -Jesus Christ is my personal Savior and Lord,
   -Christ has called me to live for His eternal purposes rather than for temporal gains (2 Corinthians 4:17-18; Matthew 13:44),
   -It is my commitment to go anywhere and do anything that my Lord directs me to do.

_____

Signature   Date

In view of the fact that:

-God has called me to be His ambassador (2 Corinthians 5:18-20; Acts 1:8),

-All people are lost apart from Christ becoming their personal Savior and Lord (Acts 4:12),

-Jesus commands us to take the Good News of His life, death, and resurrection to all creation (Matthew 28:18-20; Mark 16:15),

-A primary hindrance to fulfilling His Great Commission is the lack of laborers willing to go (Matthew 9:37, 38),

-It is my purpose, if God so leads, to spend at least one year of my life as a missionary to help fulfill Christ's Great Commission.

Signature   Date

I'd like each of you to take a card, pray about it tonight, tomorrow, or for as long as you want. But then, if you are willing to surrender your life's plan, your parent's life plan, or anyone else's life plan to choose to fulfill the foreordained purposes of God, I'd like you to place it in a box I'll put over there.

Let's pray."

I do not recall how many students returned the revised Princeton Pledge, but a number of students signed it that first year and for several years thereafter. As a result, those who immediately went into the marketplace or grad school did so after truly wrestling with the will of God for their lives. Others spent a year in ministry after graduation, and then followed the Lord to serve Him in other capacities. Still others ended up in full-time Christian vocational ministry as pastors, missionaries, or other Christian efforts. To God be the thanks and glory!

But God had more in mind when He had me write the revised Princeton Pledge than simply sharing it with Princeton students. The next chapter reveals God's greater purposes.

Chapter 36

THE MILLENNIAL PLEDGE

About four weeks after the Ski Safari, I was in Germany attending a conference for the **W**orldwide **S**tudent **N**etwork Regional Directors (which was now my regional title) and ministry leaders from around the world. During one of the sessions, only the WSN leaders, along with a few other campus ministry regional directors, were present.

We were seeking to look into the future, and we recognized the need for something different that might inspire the students' sense of vision, something to challenge them to respond in greater numbers to Christ's lordship. The two people who were passionate about this idea were Keith, the Worldwide Student Network Director from the Great Lakes Region, and Sam who was also on the Great Lakes Regional Directors team.

As I heard what they said, I immediately commented that at the end of January, God had put something on my heart as I was challenging the Princeton students. I still had a couple of the cards of the revised Princeton Pledge in my Bible, and I pulled them out and gave it to them to read.

"**This is it! This is it!**" one of them said enthusiastically. As others read the revised Princeton Pledge, they chimed in, "This is **exactly** what we were thinking about." As the conversation continued, there was a sense that we were jumping onto a train that God would be driving. Shortly thereafter, we were calling the challenge the Millennial Pledge.

The Mid-Atlantic Region and the Great Lakes Region were the early adapters to using the Millennial Pledge. In the fall of 1997, the Great Lakes Region (Cru) presented the Millennial Pledge during their first gathering of student leaders. Over fifty students signed the Pledge that weekend. As the Millennial Pledge was presented at the Great Lakes Christmas Conference in December, those fifty students got on the stage and shared with the entire conference their commitment to surrender their lives to Christ and if He so led, to give at least a year of their lives in full-time missionary work. After hearing the Millennial Pledge presented, 700 students at the Great Lakes Christmas Conference signed the pledge, came forward to the front of the room, and laid their commitment at the foot of the cross which had been placed on the stage! Hundreds of other students responded in a similar way at the Philadelphia Christmas Conference.

As word of the response of students spread, the Millennial Pledge became a part of the night of surrender and challenge at Christmas conferences across the country for the next three years. Cru leadership in other countries also heard about it and asked for permission to translate it. As a result, it began to be used at other university student conferences around the world.

Prior to the Millennial Pledge, it was normal for Cru to have fifty to seventy-five Stinters (graduates who went for one to two years to help launch university student ministries around God's world) each year. After the Millennial Pledge, the number of Stinters going overseas jumped to 100, then 200, then 300 and more. The number of U.S. stateside interns also jumped, as well as the number of new Cru staff. Other students who signed the Pledge were led by God to become pastors, serve in churches, or minister through other missions agencies.

Even today, twenty years later, I am often surprised as someone comes up to me and says something like, "You probably don't know this, but I am one of those former students who signed the Millennial Pledge." An example I heard in June of 2018, is that Josh Newell, the present executive director of the *JESUS* Film Project, a film on the life of Jesus that is being seen all over the world, was one of the 700 who signed the Millennial Pledge at the Great Lakes Winter Conference.

I am humbled and amazed as I think about what happened.

As I humbled myself before God and prayed on my knees that snowy night in Vermont, God chose to guide my thoughts. I wrote what was intended to be heard by eighty Princeton students, but God had thousands of students all over His world on His mind. Isaiah 55:8-9 says, "For My thoughts are not your thoughts, nor are your ways My ways, declares the LORD. For as the heavens are higher than the earth, so are My ways higher than your ways, and My thoughts than your thoughts." It is not that we seek to be great, but that we humbly seek a great God. To **God be the glory**!

THE MILLENNIAL PLEDGE

In view of the fact that:

☑ God created me uniquely & wonderfully for His purposes, which He prepared for me before I was born, (Psalm 139:1-18, Eph 2:10)

☑ Jesus Christ is my personal Savior and Lord,

☑ Christ has called me to live for His eternal purposes rather than living for temporal gains, (2 Cor. 4:17-18, Matt. 13:44)

it is my commitment to go anywhere and do anything that my Lord directs me to do.

_____

Signature   Date

In view of the fact that:

☑ God has called me to be His Ambassador, (2 Cor. 5:18-20, Acts 1:8)

☑ All people are lost apart from Christ becoming their personal Savior and Lord, (Acts 4:12)

☑ Jesus commands us to take the Good News of His life, death, & resurrection to all creation, (Matt. 28:18-20, Mark 16:15)

☑ The primary hindrance to fulfilling His Great Commission is a lack of laborers willing to go,

it is my commitment, if God so leads, to spend at least one year of my life as a missionary to help fulfill Christ's Great Commission.

_____

Signature   Date

The Millenial Pledge Card

Chapter 37

700 *JESUS* DVDs SMUGGLED

————◦∝◦————

"Your Lives are the Most Expendable!"

T he DVDs had each been carefully and colorfully wrapped as gifts in thick gold wrapping paper. Seven hundred copies of the *JESUS* film in the native language were about to be taken into this communist country in Asia. Hidden underneath pieces of clothing, about seventy DVDs were placed in the luggage of each of the ten travelers. Though I had taken a smaller number of DVDs into this country on previous trips, what we were doing this time was totally different, and it was scary.

If one of us was stopped and the seventy DVDs found, it would be seen as an intentional act on the person's part to smuggle banned information into the country.

If one person was caught, would all of us be caught? What would be the consequences? Would the materials be taken by the authorities and the person or the group still be free to enter the country? Would they take the materials and require us to return to the States on the next flight? Would they interrogate us? Would they imprison us for a short period of time?

We didn't know. It had been a few years since someone had been caught smuggling things into the country, so no one really knew. We hoped for the best, prayed, and trusted that God in His sovereignty would guide our steps.

Our plane arrived. After gathering our luggage, we individually walked towards the searching stations where the authorities randomly pulled people aside to go through their bags. One by one, while praying non-stop, team members walked by the officers without being searched. As I approached the guards, just ahead of me some people were pulled to the side. I walked through without being stopped. "Whew, thank you Lord!" There was one team member behind me. Looking past the guards, avoiding eye contact, and attempting to look calm while his heart raced with fear, he passed through. At that moment, with my heart pounding, my emotions began shaking within me with thankfulness and joy to God. Relief enveloped me. All of us had made it through customs without our luggage being searched. The first step in giving 700 university students the *JESUS* film in their own language had been accomplished.

Prior to leaving the U.S., as a team we discussed the process of entering the country, the fact that in the hotel, our bags would be searched by maids, and that we might be followed. We rehearsed what should or shouldn't be said if one of us was stopped by the police. The first part of the trip had been fulfilled successfully, but much more was yet ahead of us.

The goal of this trip was to "push and test the boundaries" of what could be done to get the Good News into the hands of university students. We were seeking to meet students whom others would never reach.

We traveled to the hotel. Each day, a couple people would stay behind at the hotel in the rooms where all the DVDs were stashed to ensure that the DVDs would not be found.

The plan was to divide into groups of two or three. Each group would travel each day to two or three new universities. We would attempt to walk past the guards at the entrance of each university with confidence, as if we were there with some form of official approval. Once inside the university campus, we would ask students where the male student dorms were. We walked into the dorm, and asked any student we met, "Do you or does anyone here speak English?" Without fail, they would take us to the room of a student who could speak English. Within minutes, the room would be filled with seven, ten, or more students. The plan was to ask them questions about their country, what it was like being a university student, allow them to ask us one or two questions about America, and then leave within twenty minutes. But, before we left, we said that we would like to give each of them a gift from America. We handed out the gift-wrapped *JESUS* films, walked out of the dorm, headed to another dorm or two, and then would leave campus. To avoid being caught by the authorities, we would only stay on each campus for about an hour.

A number of the teams were stopped at the entrance of a few universities. The explanation of why we were there was that we were from universities in America, and were there to meet students at the school. Sometimes the team would be admitted and other times they were asked to leave. Fortunately, none of the teams were pulled aside and interrogated.

In the days that followed, each of the 700 *JESUS* films was given to a university student. At the end of the film, if someone wanted further information, they were given an Internet site that went out of the country. This center would keep track of the number of requests for information, provide answers to questions, and offer follow-up materials. We had been told that if one of the students viewed the film, they usually shared it with about seven other students or family members. If this occurred, through our efforts we would have:

-given the *JESUS* film to 700 university students on campuses that to our knowledge had no previous Christian evangelistic activity

-identified campuses where it was easier or more difficult for others to go in the future

-determined if such an attempt to spread the Good News would be profitable for others to attempt in the future

-and rejoiced in the fact that if each of the 700 students who received a *JESUS* film shared it with seven others, we would have exposed 5,600 people to the Gospel of Jesus Christ.

As we gathered on the last night in the country, I shared with everyone how thankful I was for them, for their courage, their trust in God, and their willingness to be interrogated without knowing what the full outcome would be. I lauded them with the significance of what we believed was accomplished. How, together, they had pushed out the boundaries of what might be done in the future.

After a pause I added, "We were particularly thankful for what had been learned through their efforts. We attempted what we did because, since they would only be in the country ten days, we considered "their lives to be the most expendable."

Eyes shot open, jaws dropped, and a "What?" came flying out of one student's mouth.

Seeing their shock and surprise, I kind of smirked and said, in a way, it was true. The safety of those who stay longer or have more contact with national believers is more of a concern. As a result, we would never ask those individuals to do what you have done. But I also told them that we didn't do anything that we thought would put them or the ministry in serious jeopardy. Whether in the midst of their shock they heard those last words, I do not know.

What I do know is that God used this team and this new effort to pave the way for future daring efforts to spread the Good News.

Chapter 38

THE SLEEPLESS NIGHT

————⚬————

The knock on the door seemed urgent. Accompanying it was an anxiously whispered, "Ron." It was 10pm and everyone had gone to their rooms for the night. A little surprised, I opened the door and there stood Susan (not her real name), a woman who along with other key leaders from our region traveled with me to a country in Asia on a shorter missions trip.

"I can't find it, I can't find it," she exclaimed with fear and dread in her tone.

"Can't find what?" I asked.

"My notes!"

"What notes?"

"The notes I took about the ministry. All the names, all the campuses, all that God is doing!"

"What!" I said "I told you if you took notes, you always had to keep them in your possession!"

"I know, I know," she said, "but I thought that was only while we were in the previous city"

"What? I never said only there."

We had traveled to another city and after moving into our hotel rooms, left for the day to visit tourist sites. Throughout the trip, I had reminded everyone many times that their bags could be looked through by the maids and that nothing of significance should be left behind. Unfortunately, Susan didn't catch the significance of or follow what I said.

I said, "Please, go back to your room, look through your suitcase and all your belongings again, and again, and again."

"I've already looked through my suitcase three times," she responded.

"Susan, this is serious business. Right now it doesn't matter how many times you have looked through it. Look through everything again, and let me know if you find the notes."

The door closed and immediately I began to consider what my next steps should be.

Should I bring everyone together right away to let them know about the situation and begin to go through interrogation training?

Should I wait longer to see if Susan returned to say she found her notes?

Should I think through things more comprehensively, so that when I pulled everyone together, I would have completely thought through everything that should be said and how I should say it?

Some members of the team had already gone to bed after a long day of walking. As I sat there praying, thinking, wrestling through the options, I decided to give Susan more time.

Minutes, a half hour, an hour passed. But Susan didn't return. It was 11pm. I decided to go to bed.

Question, after question rolled through my mind as I tossed and turned in bed, unable to sleep.

Who had gotten into her room and taken the notes?

To which authorities had they been given?

Had the contents already been passed on to the authorities in the previous city?

Were our key people in that city going to be pulled in for interrogation the next day?

Would our entire ministry and years of efforts be undermined by this information?

In the sleepless hours, my plan developed for gathering the team the next morning, leaving the hotel, going to a park where we could talk without others hearing, and where I would provide the interrogation training on how to respond to various questions and accusations. I would also ask everyone to join me in serious prayer and fasting. The night was long, sleepless, and spent in continuous prayer.

In the morning, my heart was troubled and yet in a strange way, also at peace in terms of what I needed to do from that point forward.

At 7am I heard someone walking down the hard wooden floor of the hallway. A knock on the door caused fear to rise up within me.

Oh no*! Were the authorities here already? I hadn't had time to gather and brief everyone? We* **weren't ready** *to be interrogated!*

Filled with apprehension, I opened the door.

"I found it! I found it! I just wanted you to know first thing," Susan shared excitedly.

Relieved, yet perplexed I asked, "When did you find it?"

"Oh, about twenty minutes after I came to your door."

"**What**?" I exclaimed. "I've been awake all night, wrestling through every possible scenario and possible outcome. Why didn't you let me know when you found it?"

"Oh, I'm sorry," she said. "I thought you might be asleep by then."

"**Ahhh**," I groaned in disbelief. "Thanks for letting me know."

God had some lessons for Susan and for me through this situation. For her, it was to truly listen and follow the instructions of her leadership. For me, it was to find my rest in Him, to rely on His faithfulness despite our circumstances.

Chapter 39

I Finally Got It!

———————⚬⚬———————

I t is often said that "one's greatest strength can also contribute towards his greatest weakness." I believe this was true for me. I am sad to say that it took God a long time to teach me more about myself, more about His gracious kindness, His plan, and His patience towards me. Most likely, there is more teaching yet to come.

Though you may not emotionally "get it" at a young age, or even feel the need into your twenties, my hope is that you will be wiser than I was, and apply this aspect of God's wisdom and plan for your lives much sooner than I did.

There is a side to your Granddad that is downright lazy. However, my goal orientation, passion for God, passion for ministry, and passion to fulfill every purpose God has for my life usually override this "lazy" tendency. As a result, I have been willing to undertake almost anything, **if** I believed God was leading me to do it.

In 2002, Matt, who for many years had been the Cru Director at Princeton University, felt led by the Lord to leave Cru staff and to launch a ministry of his own. Matt is a gifted leader whose family is filled with entrepreneurs. Launching new businesses seemed to be within the family DNA.

Within Cru, we wanted Matt to try his innovative ideas and methods within our organizational structure. However, he felt that ultimately, some of our ministry policies would inhibit him from doing everything he desired. The vision for his ministry launch was to begin a new and unique ministry to all of the Ivy League schools, beginning at Princeton. God has blessed his efforts, and he was right in concluding that he would not have been able to do some of the things that he has within the Cru ministry.

However, one unfortunate circumstance associated with Matt's departure was that he informed us of his decision to leave Cru staff in May. Within the ministry of Cru, as regional directors, we made our leadership and campus director placement assignments for the following year in March, so strategic ministry planning for the next school year could occur in April. After we heard he was leaving the ministry in May, as a regional director team, we challenged several experienced campus directors to move and step into the role at Princeton. Unfortunately, by May, they had already prayed, made plans, and were passionate about what they felt God was leading them to believe Him to do at their present campuses for the next school year. Thus, they all turned down the opportunity to move to Princeton.

At the time of Matt's departure, Grandmom had been fulfilling the role of overseeing the women's side of the ministry at Princeton for a number of years and was committed to continuing in this role.

Because I didn't want all the responsibility of overseeing the entire Princeton ministry to fall on Grandmom, with the approval of the National WSN Leadership and our regional team, it was decided that I would continue as the Regional WSN Director, but also assume the responsibilities of the campus director for the next year.

I knew from the start this would be a daunting task. Over ten years prior to this, the combined roles of an area director and a campus director had been attempted. Four of us were excited to test out the feasibility of this new job. One director lasted one year and found it to be too overwhelming. Two guys lasted two years and determined the scope was too great. I lasted three years and knew my situation had to change. Fortunately, during those three years, I had prepared one of our staff men, Scott, to take over as the campus director at Princeton.

The role and responsibilities of a regional director were both different and significantly greater than that of the former area director. Under the previous area structure, there were twenty areas in the country. Under the regional structure, there were ten regions. Rather than the New York-New Jersey Area existing, now all the universities in six states became the Mid-Atlantic Region. Thus, the geographical scope tripled in size. With the increase in scope, the roles and job descriptions to accomplish everything changed. The WSN (Worldwide Student Network) role came into existence in the new regional structure, with the focus of responsibility being designing, developing, and executing the mobilization of Cru staff and students within the region to participate in seven-to-ten-day vision trips and international summer mission projects. However, over time, the WSN responsibilities morphed into overseeing not just the vision trips and summer projects, but also the sending, training, personal development, and the ministry effectiveness of Stint teams(graduates going for one to two years to launch university student movements overseas) for our partnership locations. As the number of students who signed The Millennial Pledge grew every year, the number of international partnerships grew from two to three to four to five to six, and eventually to seven international locations around the world for the Mid-Atlantic Region! To God be the praise! **But**, this also meant my responsibilities had increased exponentially! In addition, oversight for the mobilization of long-term staff and developing relationships with key international Cru leaders in our partnership countries around the world also became a part of the job.

Everyone who knew anything about pulling off the regional/international job and simultaneously leading well on the local level knew it would be nearly impossible. It was understood both nationally and regionally that a decline in some aspects of ministry effectiveness would have to be embraced. The national leadership, regional leadership, and I viewed this one year as being a season for me to accept more responsibilities than would be prudent.

As my personal vision for Princeton University was renewed, I loved the challenge and was motivated to the hilt. I loved the students, the staff team, and what God was doing. To pull off both responsibilities, I determined that on Monday, Tuesday, and Wednesday, I would do the regional job. On Wednesday night, Thursday, and Friday, I would do the Princeton job. I was pretty good at mentally compartmentalizing responsibilities, so I thought this might work. As needed, both jobs required time over the weekends.

I was not afraid of hard work, I was motivated, plus, I would be helping Char continue to do what she loved in ministering to the women students.

As the days and weeks passed, several changes began to take place in my life. Trying to stay on top of both jobs made the list of responsibilities never-ending. I would work from the moment I got up in the morning till dinner time (most lunches were meetings), take a break for dinner and down time from 5:30-7:30, and then usually work until 11:30pm. Despite this regimen, I found that at least four nights a week, I would wake up between 3-3:30am with several important items on my mind that I hadn't had time to think about the day before. To me, the great thing was that God knew I hadn't thought about these things, so He would wake me up. I would write them on a pad I had next to my bed, and go back to sleep. I rejoiced in the knowledge that God was guiding my mind in the night watches.

Unfortunately, as time passed, rather than being able to immediately go back to sleep, I began to toss and turn, unable to get different issues off my mind.

Then a second consequence of trying to stay on top of all the responsibilities began.

I began to experience pain in my right jaw. The process of God revealing hidden, unrecognized concerns began.

I can vividly remember the first time this occurred. I was riding in my car towards the Princeton campus. It was a "Princeton day" and the pain in my jaw was fairly strong. I began to pray, "God, why do I have this pain? Is this due to stress? Is there something bothering me below the surface that I am consciously unaware?" As soon as I finished praying, three issues immediately popped into my head. Two of the issues were related to my regional job, and one was related to Princeton. I can see myself saying something like, "God, thanks for revealing these issues to me. But this is a Princeton day. I cannot do a thing about the regional situations. You are just going to have to take care of it, or, make it possible for things to be okay until Monday. I know what I can do about the Princeton situation. Thanks for letting me know what was going on emotionally inside of me."

As I continued to drive to campus, my awareness of the pain continued. However, about twenty minutes later, the thought came to my mind, *Hey, the pain is gone.* I prayed a very grateful, "Thanks, God."

Gradually, I discerned one of the reasons this occurred stemmed directly from my ability to compartmentalize and mentally shift from one job to the other. On Wednesday night, my mind became so focused on the Princeton ministry, mentally my regional job could have been non-existent. The problem was the shift was only mental, and not emotional. I had no idea what I was or wasn't carrying with me emotionally from the other job. Over time, I realized what bothered me was never related to ministry details.

Rather, it was people-related concerns and needs that weren't getting addressed that emotionally affected me.

God clearly knew what was happening.

In His goodness, He simply let me feel the pain, opened my mind to the concerns I was carrying with me that I didn't know existed, gave me the opportunity to pray and release the problems back to Him, and then He took the pain away. It amazed me how 99 percent of the time, twenty to thirty minutes after I prayed, the pain was gone.

Over the rest of that first year, I consistently saw this pattern occur in my life. As the days, weeks, and months passed though, I increasingly realized that continuing this way would not be good in the long term. Unfortunately, as a regional team, we were not able to identify another campus director for Princeton. As a result, the one-year season for the two jobs evolved into a two-year season, which then expanded to a three-year season.

As the time carrying the two jobs continued, I had the "Perfect Storm" variables for an emotional breakdown. For me, that means someone has been dealing with so many problems, for so long, his mind and body begin to shut down. He is unable to think, act, and respond like he normally would.

Though I knew I couldn't explain it, I knew I was in emotional trouble. I began to wrestle with God, asking, "How am I going to make it?"

As I was reading the Word one day, I once again read about the Sabbath. God worked for six days, and on the seventh day He rested. In being like Him, in identifying with Him, He commanded the Israelites to take a twenty-four-hour period for rest and restoration with Him every week. As I read this, my heart groaned, "God, I have not been listening to You. How many times have I read about a Sabbath Day of rest and renewal each week?" I knew immediately that for the first time in my life, to **survive**, I needed to take His command seriously.

That day, a new appreciation for the love, care, design, and concern God has for us began to take root. For over fifty years, I had not taken God's design for us as man seriously. I had not appreciated His love or wisdom in commanding us to set aside this day for Him.

In Genesis we read that God worked for six days, and on the seventh day, He rested. Did God rest on the seventh day because He was tired, exhausted from all His creative work? No, God does not get tired. HE was not in need of rest. Yet on the seventh day, He made this day holy — different from the previous six days. (Just so you know, in my comments above and in what follows, I am not entering the debate on whether the days of Genesis Chapter 1 were literal twenty-four-hour periods of time, or ages. Rather, my purpose is to focus on the seven days of a week for us as man and God's instructions for us regarding the Sabbath).

In Mark 2:27 the Scriptures say, "Jesus said to them, 'The Sabbath was made for man, and not man for the Sabbath.'" In His comment, Jesus didn't limit the Sabbath created for man to the Israelites. God set aside the seventh day for the benefit of "man," all mankind, which included me.

Recently I heard a story about a woman who was going to have a baby. Her doctor told her that if she did not have complete bed rest, her life could be in danger, and her baby might also die. She took what the doctor said pretty seriously, but at the time, she continued to lead a Bible study, which she thought wouldn't be bad. At her next appointment, the doctor asked her if she was staying in bed. She said yes, except for the Bible study. She said it didn't seem to adversely affect her in any way. The doctor said, "I don't care whether you feel any different or not, you are putting your life and the life of that baby in danger." Whether the mother felt the need for continuous bedrest was not the issue. For her own good and the baby's, she needed rest. For me, it shouldn't have mattered whether I felt the need for a day of rest. God created me, knows me better than I know myself, and the wise choice would have been to follow His instructions.

As I changed my ways and diligently began to observe a Sabbath rest once a week, I found myself renewed spiritually, emotionally, mentally, and physically. It enabled me, I believe, to avoid an emotional breakdown that was just around the corner. I am sincerely thankful that our Heavenly Father is intimately acquainted with all of our ways and that He knew His instructions regarding the Sabbath was what I needed.

Apart from the need for physical, emotional, mental, and spiritual rest and restoration, God had another significant purpose behind this command regarding the Sabbath.

Ezekiel 20:12 states, "Also, I gave them My sabbaths to be a sign between Me and them, that they might know that I am the LORD who sanctifies them."

Ezekiel 20:20 says, "Sanctify My sabbaths; and they shall be a sign between Me and you, that you may know that I am the LORD your God."

It took faith for the Jewish people to choose to work only six days, when the people from other countries and religions would work seven days. I have become convinced it is the same for us. If we choose to keep a Sabbath day, that forces us to trust God to make up the difference. It sanctifies, stretches, and strengthens our faith in **Him** in very practical ways every week. It truly enables us to know that **He** is "the Lord your God."

I pray that your Grandmom, I, and our families will grow in our faith and glorify God by recognizing God's example and His purposes for the Sabbath. That we would grow in our appreciation for how He designed us as man to function best: mentally, emotionally, physically, and spiritually.

I pray we will become men and women with a growing faith; those who will trust God to do more in six days than would normally be accomplished in seven days of work, or for you as students, studying, etc. This is one of the ways God has chosen to enable us to "know that He is the LORD" each week.

I pray we will enjoy grasping how He desires to sanctify us, as we observe the Sabbath day and make it holy.

(Note: Given the multiple biblical purposes for the Sabbath, I do not believe a specific day of the week for its observance is critical. Saturday is the day the Israelites observed the Sabbath. In order to give focus to the day Jesus resurrected, the early church fathers chose Sunday to become the day of rest. For pastors and sometimes others, Sunday is definitely not a day rest, but a day of work for which they get paid. Thus I believe another day of the week would be applicable in their situation.)

Chapter 40

HAVE HIS HEART

————◇————

The traffic was minimal as I drove home on Interstate 295 from our Cru regional staff conference. I was wrestling in my mind over comments our staff made during a special meeting I led during the conference. I began praying something like, "God, what should we do? How can we change things so that our movements become more like You would want them to be? God, please guide my thoughts? You know what we should do. Just guide me."

A month earlier, I had been at a conference in North Carolina where I heard other Global Missions Regional Directors (no longer called Worldwide Student Network Regional Directors) share things that enabled their campuses to have a greater vision for reaching God's world with the Good News. As I gathered the small group of staff at our regional conference, I explained how the Mid-South and Great Lakes Regions were doing things. I asked if we could adapt and apply them on our campuses.

The resounding and consistent feedback was, "We can't do things that way. It won't work. We do not have large staff teams like those other regions. Our staff have contact with students on multiple campuses with small movements. Trying to do things the way the Mid-South and Great Lakes Regions do it, just will not work."

I was discouraged and at a loss. I knew the insights the staff had shared were correct, and yet, now I was left with no plan of how we should proceed. They had said what we needed was a plan that would be led by vision-filled, motivated student leadership. But how could we get there?

As I continued to drive up I-295, all of a sudden, a flurry of thoughts rushed into my mind:

We are starting at the wrong place. We shouldn't start with the goal, we need to start with the heart.

If the hearts of the students are in the right place, then the motivation, vision, and outcomes will follow.

We need for students to get God's heart, His perspective.

We need to ask the question, 'Do we have a heart with the passions of His heart?'

We should start with a teaser campaign at the student winter conference. Something that will flash before the students' eyes.

Thoughts were flooding my mind, but I was driving and nothing was getting written down. I could not lose this moment. I had to stop the car.

At that very moment, a rest area exit sign appeared (isn't God's timing cool? He thinks of everything). I pulled into the rest area, pulled out my computer, and began to record the somewhat discombobulated, disjointed array of thoughts bouncing into my mind from all directions.

As I continued to write thoughts down, simultaneously other questions and issues emerged in my mind:

Should we try to pull this off at the Winter Conference less than a month away?

How can I gain the help I need to put together a video, design, and order t-shirts?

The "Got His Heart for His World" phrase is too long. We need another way of saying it.

This will cause havoc amongst the conference team.

To pull this off, I would have to ask for so many favors, it would take me years to make it up to others!

Does God want me to do this?

"God, do You want me to do this now?"

A lot had to be done, and had to be done soon.

It was Tuesday afternoon before Thanksgiving. All the staff in the Mid-Atlantic Region were traveling to their families or their homes to celebrate Thanksgiving. When I got home, I needed to help Grandmom with our own Thanksgiving preparations. **No one** would appreciate an urgent e-mail or phone call about a **crazy** idea right now.

"God, what do You want me to do, and when?" was my prayer as I drove out of the rest area towards home for Thanksgiving.

Friday morning after Thanksgiving I sent an e-mail to Matt, my associate Global Missions regional director, and Rachael, the regional media and communications team leader. I briefly shared what occurred on my ride home from the staff conference and asked if we could meet the following Tuesday to discuss my thoughts and ideas.

We began our meeting on Tuesday the only way I could imagine beginning such a critical discussion: in surrendered, heartfelt, humble prayer for God's guidance, wisdom, and direction. I began by admitting what I was about to share might seem a bit unusual. My thoughts were incomplete, a lot of holes existed, with innumerable unanswered questions, but that was why we were meeting. I told them I believed the Lord was behind the basic ideas and I needed their insights, wisdom, and expertise as other parts of the Body. But I also said with a great sense of conviction that I was willing to do whatever it might take in terms of effort, time, the asking of favors, financial cost, even the potential loss of any positive reputation I might have to do this, **if** I continued to sense this was God's leading.

What a blessing it is to benefit from others who love God, have different gifts, and want what God wants. At the end of Tuesday's meeting, several decisions were made with a unanimous agreement among us. The greatest decision was that it would be wiser to wait till next year's Winter Conference to implement the ideas.

A year and four weeks after the initial ideas began to flow, excitement, concern that the video/sound/timing, etc. would happen as planned, and virtually non-stop prayer enveloped me as the unveiling of "Have His Heart" was about to occur. What would God do?

As God answered this question, two significant thoughts emerged in my mind.

The first was that I am more convinced than ever that the foremost desire of my life needs to be to walk closely, intimately connected, to my loving, living God. We never know when He might have a greater, bigger, unanticipated way to work in our lives than we would ever expect. Whether it is a "Get out of the tent and into the car" moment, a Millennial Pledge, or just a moment in which we sense His power and presence in a more personal way, these are the moments we do not want to miss in life. To walk with **Him**, to know **Him**, to fulfill every purpose He has for us, to **Have His Heart** is our greatest privilege.

Second, God chose to cause a significant response in the lives of the students at the conference that day and night. At a special meeting that began at 10pm while a concert and other entertaining activities were occurring, over 10 percent of the students at the conference made a commitment to seek to be transformed themselves to Have His Heart for His World, and to be a Have His Heart ambassador on their campus. They agreed to be the point person who would encourage one minute to be taken at every Cru meeting, every Bible study, and every prayer meeting every week to offer a praise for answered prayer, to read a "God Story," or to share a prayer request from around God's world.

After hearing about how God worked during the Mid-Atlantic Winter Conference, National Global Missions leadership asked me to share what we did at our national meetings in March. As a result, several other regions in the country began to use the same strategy in their regions the next year. It was exciting as we saw students get excited over the next several years about encouraging students on their campus to **Have His Heart**.

Though the long-term effect of this effort didn't expand to every region in the U.S., nor fulfill some of the results I had hoped, I was thankful I had listened to the Lord, I had followed what I felt He wanted me to do, and that for every student affected, if they gained *His Heart for His World*, it was worth every bit of effort.

My prayer for myself, for you, for all God's children is that we would *Have His Heart for His World*.

Chapter 41

THOUGHTS FROM MY HEART

————————✕————————

I–God's Design: How He Created Me – How He Created You

W hy do you look the way you look, think the way you think, laugh the way you laugh, run the way you run? In part, it is because you are the only person who has **ever lived** who has the DNA, the same physical make up that you do.

Psalm 139:13-16 says:

> For You formed my inward parts, You knitted me together in my mother's womb. I praise You, for I am fearfully and wonderfully made. Wonderful are Your works; my soul knows it very well. My frame was not hidden from You when I was being made in secret, intricately woven in the depths of the earth. Your eyes saw my unformed substance; in Your book were written, every one of them, the days that were formed for me, when as yet there was none of them. (ESV)

My hope and prayer is that as you live your life, you will increasingly realize you are uniquely and wonderfully made. As

King David declared 3,000 years ago in the verses above, and as modern science has now confirmed, no one else is just like you. Yet for most of us, there are times when we wish we were someone else. We look at others and wish we had the physical appearance, intelligence, athletic ability, personality, or the humor someone else has. I know this has been true for me. No one else can ever be you. If you are not you, who will be?

One of the greatest gifts we can receive in life is to know that we do not have to be like someone else to be special, to have value, to have purposes which God has chosen for us that are different from anyone else He has ever created.

In addition to our natural physical characteristics and abilities which come through our DNA, Ephesians 2:10 says, "For we are His workmanship, created in Christ Jesus for good works, which God prepared beforehand so that we would walk in them." 1 Corinthians 12:7 states, "But to each one is given the manifestation of the Spirit for the common good." 1 Corinthians 12:11 continues by saying, "But one and the same Spirit works all these things, distributing to each one individually just as He wills." 1 Peter 4:10 declares, "As each one has received a special gift, employ it in serving one another, as good stewards of the manifold grace of God." Imagine that, as we became born again Christians, God caused additional "workmanship," new gifting, and new purposes to be added to our lives.

One thing that can be said of your Granddad: there is no one like him, including the good and the not so good. Though other people have traits similar to mine, when you put me all together, I am one of a kind, and that goes beyond how I look. Traits that I have gradually realized are true about me include:

I like Variety — the changing seasons; the many shapes of faces as I walk down the streets of NYC energize me; I love new situations and circumstances, a different schedule every day. At times,

I even find myself shaving my face differently, just to make sure I am not getting into a rut.

I like being Spontaneous — having my backpack with me while I was in college just in case an opportunity to go somewhere opened up; meeting new people and seeing where a conversation might take us; deciding in the moment with your Grandmom whether to go to NYC or Washington, D.C. one afternoon when we were sitting on the beach in Ocean City (oh, we didn't tell you about that one, did we?); traveling until we feel tired and stopping at the nearest hotel rather than having everything planned out (this trait wasn't always the best when your mom was growing up. I needed to listen more to Grandmom and finally did).

I am a Big Picture person rather than someone who likes to focus on the little details.

I like Pioneering new territory — being the first to try something — figuring things out as I go along.

Let me ask you, if you were to create someone like this, what kind of job, what kind of purpose would you want him to fulfill? Could it be a job where he always met new people, found himself in new and different situations, possibly in different parts of the world; in situations that no one had necessarily faced before that he could enter into and figure out the best directions to take?

Yes, exactly! And that is what has been true for my life.

I haven't always known what I now know to be true about myself. But God did. Gradually as I followed **Him** day by day, year by year, He led me into the various circumstances and job paths that enabled me to fulfill His purposes. God's path for my life has been 100 percent consistent with how He designed me.

Before you were born, God thought, *Let me make a boy or girl who will be exactly like you are. Then, when you place (or will place) your faith in Me as Lord and Savior, I will make you even better and more complete. I will fill you with My love, joy, peace, patience, kindness, goodness, faithfulness, and self-control (the*

Fruit of the Spirit); I will give you special spiritual gifts and abilities to glorify Me; I will also give you special "good works" for you to fulfill as you walk with Me and follow Me.

You have been given the greatest privilege anyone could ever fathom: being able to fulfill the special, unique roles and purposes that God created for you before you were born.

My prayer is that you would realize how wonderful you are, how wonderfully you have been made, and how wonderful, fulfilling, challenging, hard, yet amazing it is to get to the end of this life and say, "Oh, the amazing life that I have lived on this earth." And then to think of the exciting adventure you have waiting, to live with God forever, continuing to fulfill His purposes and the roles He has for you after you depart from this life and this earth.

"God, I can't wait to see all that You have planned for me, our family, and our grandkids!"

II–Giving towards the Lord's Work–Three Girls, Three Educations, Three Weddings

A great privilege that God has given your Grandmom and me, in addition to giving Him our hearts and following Him in the various good works He has for us vocationally, at church, etc., is to give back financially to Him for the good of others and His glory. Since your Grandmom and I individually began walking with our Heavenly Father, we both have wanted to give back to God at least a tithe (10 percent) of the money we were paid.

After we got married, we began to pray the prayer, "God, how much (what percentage) of the money we receive do You want us to give back to You?"

The Old Testament guideline for giving back to the Lord was 10 percent, being the "first fruits of your labor," regardless of the source of that income.

In the New Testament, Jesus lauded the widow who had given at one moment, "all that she had," out of her devotion to the Lord. For us, in our devotion to the Lord, we wanted our giving back to the Lord to be through Him personally leading us, rather than simply accepting what might be the automatic 10 percent plan of the Old Testament. As a result, we went to God and said, "Lord, please lead us to know how much You want us to give towards Your work."

Within a few months of being married, we felt impressed to give 15 percent of everything we received back to the Lord. Even during the difficult days in Oklahoma when we were receiving short paychecks, we gave 15 percent out of what we received. For us, to veer from this commitment was non-negotiable. We felt this was part of the "good works which God prepared beforehand" that we should do.

You may remember from Chapter 20 the situation when I was totally discouraged and for the first time I "saw" Malachi 3:10. There God says to those in the nation of Israel, " 'Bring the whole tithe into the storehouse, so that there may be food in My house, and test Me now in this', says the LORD of hosts, 'if I will not open for you the windows of heaven and pour out for you a blessing until it overflows.' " After I read that verse, in a special way, God filled me with His peace and an assurance that He would do something to provide for our needs. In part, I had confidence this would occur because I knew we had continued to give the "tithe" mentioned for Israel, in the form of the 15 percent we had felt led to give, even in our own dire financial situation.

In our marriage, we believe God has continued to lead us as we have continued to ask Him, "Lord how much, for whose needs, and in which ways do You want us to give back to You?"

For many people this may seem foolish and even irresponsible. I admit, at times it did not make our circumstances the easiest for us as a couple, or even for our girls. There were consequences to our actions. Yet, God always provided enough money for your mom—for our family, to be clothed and to do the most important things in life. Your mom didn't necessarily have the best quality, or name brands in clothing or other items but she also wasn't lacking. God **always** proved **Himself faithful** to provide so we had all we truly needed and often even above and beyond.

As your mom was growing up, your Grandmom and I specifically asked God to provide and guide us in the stewardship of the money we received, so none of our girls would have so much debt from college loans that they would be prevented from going into full-time Christian vocational ministry, if that was the direction they believed God was leading them. God, through more than a dozen different means, provided so none of our girls graduated from college with any debt. If you were to look at our income and what the costs were associated with three out-of-state college educations, it just doesn't add up. Yes, all the girls worked part time while in college, received scholarships in varying amounts, and also saved money from their summer earnings. And I believe God led Grandmom and me to be wise stewards of money that came our way. But, the numbers still do not add up. What I do know is, God orchestrated the circumstances to **totally** exceed our hopes and expectations. Our girls didn't graduate with limited debt, they graduated with no debt!

In addition to three college educations, we also had three weddings to host. **Not** an inexpensive endeavor, no matter how you do it! Once again, God in various and unusual ways provided for the weddings.

For Michelle's wedding, we were able to have the rehearsal dinner at the home of two very special friends. The wedding and reception occurred at our church. Many friends from church jumped in to help us with all the preparations, including making the cake and obtaining a catering service at a very good price. Kevin's parents (Michelle's future in-laws) were also very generous as they helped with expenses.

In all the years we were involved in ministry at Princeton University, there were only two years we had interns from Princeton Seminary working with Cru. Guess what? The two years that Kristi and Jen got married were the two years we had interns. Because students from the seminary were associated with our ministry those specific years, we were able to use their very nice dining facilities for both receptions. The seminary charged us the normal price for banquets instead of the increased $15-$20 a plate cost that is normal for wedding receptions. Additionally, because it was a seminary, we didn't have to pay any tax. The result was that thousands of dollars in normal costs were eliminated for both weddings. Coincidence? I do not think so.

I share these things with you to encourage you in two ways as you consider how you think about and manage the money God places in your hands in the future

The first is for you to know that **God is faithful**. If you "...seek first His Kingdom and His righteousness, all these things will be added to you." (Matthew 6:33) God will provide for all your needs so you can fulfill every desire and purpose He has for you.

Second, we would like to encourage you to personally seek God's guidance as you give back to Him. If He wants you to give the tithe of 10 percent, He can confirm that to you. There is absolutely nothing wrong with this. But, if He wants you to give back more, please do not cheat yourself from experiencing what could be an increased sense of His guidance and His astounding faithfulness. At times, God might lead you to do what could be viewed as foolish or unwise from a human and practical standpoint. 2 Corinthians 9:8 says, "And God is able to make All Grace abound to you, so that always having All Sufficiency in Everything, you may have an abundance for Every good deed." (capitalizations mine.) Thus, if God desires for you to give in an unexpected way to fulfill a "good work," He will work things out in the end.

One of the greatest joys that your Grandmom and I take with us into every day is the knowledge that we have sought **Him**, given back what He has led us to give, and have hopefully fulfilled the "good works which God prepared beforehand" for us through giving. We have already seen some of you, our grandchildren, giving generously towards the needs of others. For this we are very thankful. We also know that your parents are great examples for you in this.

A final thought related to money comes from Proverbs 13:22, where it says, "A good man leaves an inheritance to his children's children..." (Hey, I bet that sounds like a good idea to you!) As your Grandmom and I have gone to the Lord with this verse in our minds, we have asked, "God, how do **You** want us to approach distributing the money You have provided, when we leave this life? How much money do **You** want us to designate towards Your work? How much do **You** want us to leave as an inheritance to our children, and to our grandchildren?"

In our lives and in our deaths, our foremost goal is to glorify God. We want you to know that we are living first for His eternal purposes, not for the things of this world. We would not want the inheritance we give to your parents or to you to rob either of you from recognizing and realizing your need to truly trust God for your life's provisions.

Yet, we do want to demonstrate our constant care and love for your parents and for you. We have asked God for guidance to discern how He might want us to approach this. As a result, we have set a specific maximum amount of money to be given to each of the families of our three daughters. After that amount is distributed, 100 percent of what is left will go towards the Lord's work. We have also requested that from the money you or your parents receive, at least a tithe, or any percentage to which our Heavenly Father leads, be given back towards His work and for His glory.

It is our hope that God will be glorified as this inheritance becomes a blessing to your parents, to you, and to others.

III–The Greatest Tragedy

I considered having this section be the first of the "Thoughts From My Heart." However, since this is what I consider to be the most important thought, I wanted this to be what I leave with you.

As your mom was growing up, I had one horrible recurring thought. *With all the love that I have for your mom, how tragic it would be if she never knew or experienced that love inside of her.*

This is why, in part, I tell your mom that I love her every time I see her, every time we talk on the phone, and almost every text I send her. One thing I think you remember seeing when we are together as a family is that after we pray and give thanks to God for our food, I usually "blow your mom a kiss." In every way I can, I desire to let your mom know and **experience** the reality of my love for her.

If you recall from the beginning of this book, one thing that contributed towards my rejection of God's existence was, though I had heard that God was love and loving, I never *experienced* His love. As I thought about my desire for your mom to experience my love, I recognized that God's love for her was greater than my love for her. If it was tragic for me to love your mom and her not experience it, it would be a greater tragedy if she failed be convinced of and experience God's love for her.

Unfortunately, this may be true for many kids who grow up in Christian homes and go to church. Despite the excellent efforts of your mom and dad, and the very good church you attend, it is still possible that you could grow up hearing the **Great News** of God's existence, of Jesus' sacrifice for your sins, of the personal relationship that you can have with God through faith, and yet miss out on a true relationship with Him. Rather than thinking about God and connecting with His presence, love, and Truth, inside there could be nothing but total emptiness. As a result, you might conclude as I did, Christianity is a farce. Tragically, I know a number of kids who have grown up in Christian homes who now reject Christianity. I fear they heard and mentally knew correct facts about God, but never personally experienced His love through faith. As they think about God, a void exists.

One of the reasons I/we wrote this book to you is so you could see through the experiences of our lives how God is with us, knows every circumstance we encounter, and that through every circumstance, He wants us to walk with an awareness of His presence and the encouragement of His love within us. In Romans 5:3-8, Paul says, "And not only this, but we also exult in our tribulations, knowing that tribulation brings about perseverance, and perseverance, proven character; and proven character, hope; and hope does not disappoint, because the love of God has been poured out within our hearts through the Holy Spirit who was given to us."

My great desire, hope, and prayer for you, is that you would personally experience God's love even as I do, every day (or nearly every day). You have grown up in a Christian home and have gone to church all your life. You have heard a million times that God loves you, **but** that doesn't do you any good if you don't experience it, and know it for yourself. You will never be who you were created to be, if you do not walk with an awareness of God's presence, His guidance, or enjoy His love within you.

If the experience of God's presence and love is not something that is very real to you, then I hope you will tell your mom, your dad, your Grandmom, or me. Life is so much better when it is filled with love, and especially when it is filled with God's love. I love you **very much**. Granddad

CONCLUSION

———————⟨✕⟩———————

You did it! You have joined us in the amazing journey that our faithful heavenly Father has had for us thus far. We hope you will carry some of the stories, the emotions you felt, the challenges or encouragements you received into your own journey in life. God is all He has declared Himself to be and so much more than we can ever grasp this side of eternity.

One of Grandmom's favorite verses is Psalm 71:18: "And even when I am old and gray, O God, do not forsake me, until I declare Your strength to this generation, Your power to all who are to come." (Grandmom says she wasn't feeling particularly 'old and gray' when this verse initially resonated in her heart). This verse reflects both of our hearts as we have written this to you.

We will be filled with joy if you embrace the great privilege found in humbly walking with God, experiencing His love and presence daily, and glorifying Him as you fulfill the good works that He has prepared beforehand for your individual life.

This is the essence of the amazing journey of glorifying Him that God has had and will continue to have for us.

If you have any questions about seeking Him, loving Him, being filled with Him, experiencing His love and presence, humbly walking with Him, or glorifying Him, please let us know. (This request is given to every person who reads this book, not just our grandkids)

In Judges 2:7-10, it says that Joshua and all the generation that had entered the land had died, and verse 10b states, "and there arose another generation after them who did not know the Lord, nor yet the work which He had done for Israel." What a sad commentary on how the Israelites failed to enthrall their children with the greatness and faithfulness of God. To those of you who are not a part of our immediate family, Char and I would like to encourage you to join us in "declaring" God's work to the next generation.

If you think this book can help your children or grandchildren know the Lord or realize how fantastic it is to be able to fulfill God's purposes for their lives, please encourage them to read it even as we have with our grandkids. (whether you would go to the extent of asking them to read it four times may be a bit extreme, but who knows... ☺)

We look forward with great excitement and anticipation to the amazing journey God has yet to unfold for us and for you. To Him be all the glory, honor, and praise.

Granddad and Grandmom / Ron and Char